TRUMP MANIFESTED
Man & Overman

Compiled, Arranged, and Written
By
Joseph Freeman
Edited by Sharon Campbell

"Staring at the Sun, Certain of His Own Immensity"
© 2017 Salvador Dalí, Fundació Gala-Salvador Dalí, Artists Rights Society
Cover Design, Sharon Campbell

TRUMP MANIFESTED MAN & OVERMAN

Public Benefit Press

Copyright © 2022 by Joseph Freeman

All rights reserved. No part of this book may be used or reproduced by any means, graphic, electronic, or mechanical, including photocopying, recording, taping or by any information storage retrieval system without the written permission of the publisher.

The views expressed in this work are solely those of the author and do not necessarily reflect the views of the publisher, and the publisher hereby disclaims any responsibility for them.

ISBN: 978-0-9916103-7-2 – Electronic Version
ISBN: 978-1-7350978-5-5 – Paperback Version

Printed in the United States of America
Public Benefit Press
Date: March, 2022

"He's the great American icon!"
Trump: "Hey, why only American? Why not the world?"

Acknowledgement

I wish to express my sincerest appreciation for all those unacknowledged (though found in books, articles, and on the internet) contributors who made this book possible, who expressed their ideas related or unrelated to my own. If, for any reason, I overstepped my bounds in matters of copyright infringement, please let me know, and I will redress them in the next edition of this book. Again, thank you for your contribution to this important study of a man well worth being studied fully as possible – if any study of him could ever be fully possible. He is too much of an enigma to pinpoint as this or that; add to that, a sphinx, as well, to even know himself fully; but then who ever knows oneself fully?

CONTENTS

PREFACE	i
PURPOSE	ii

SECTION I
THE PSYCHOLOGICAL MAN

PART ONE: (Revealed by Trump Himself)	2
Character and Tactics Descriptions	3
Genius	3
Temperament	4
Appearances	9
Ego	9
Vanity	10
Revenge	11
Showmanship	12
Emotions	13
Conflict	13
Toughness	13
Racism	16
Women	16
Children	25
Honesty	26
Friendship	26
Beauty	26
Reading	27
Learning	27
Stimulants	28

Humility	28
Altruism	28
Success	29
Money/Wealth	38
Elitism	39
Business	39
Politics	43
Religion	47
Contradictions	48
PART TWO (Revealed by others and this Author)	59
Character and Tactics Descriptions	60
Favorable Perspectives	60
Unfavorable Perspectives	65
Moderate Perspectives	74
Malicious Perspectives	75
The Author's Comments Regarding the Severity of These Malicious Perspectives	75
PART THREE (Fictional Impressions of Trump's Character and Tactics Stated by Theodore Dreiser, Shakespeare, and by this Author)	79

SECTION II

TRUMP AS OVERMAN?

PART FOUR (Revealed by others and this Author)	101
The Overman and Trump	102
Nietzsche on the Overman	104
The following Selected Exemplars Related to the Overman Concept	108
Trump's Seeming Relationship to the Overman	111

SECTION III
TRUMP AS HISTORIC NECESSITY

PART FIVE (Revealed by Others and this Author)	125
Trump as Historic Necessity of Events-to-Come	126
PART SIX (Stated by Others and this Author)	150
Trump Thoughts from American Insurgent to World Emperor	
In Conclusion	166
Bibliography	
Author's professional background	

PREFACE

This study by and of Donald Trump surveys the man and his tactics in relation to his character and to his self-acclaimed man of destiny, be it as Nietzsche's overman concept or as a Napoleon or Alexander historic overlord concept.

The selected quotations in this book are mainly by Donald Trump himself and by others in relation to him, as cited verbatim from newspapers, magazines, interviews, books, internet, etc. without any alterations or padding from the author.

For the most part, this book intentionally omits the quotation sources in the text; since, I believe, they would detract from the simplicity and flow of its narrative. Nor are quotation dates or notes included; since this book is not an historical nor biographical, nor comparative, study. Nor is it intended to be a strict, scholarly, treatment in the formal sense of the word; though *factually*, *psychologically*, *philosophically*, it certainly stands as scholarly – as "the arts and sciences" meaning of the word.

PURPOSE
Who Is He? What Is He? Why Is He?

What motivated me at first to write and research this book on Donald Trump, knowing hardly anything about the man, was to pinpoint his moral and psychological character into a mold that justified the belief that he was basically a reprehensible person, somewhat of a cad; and certainly, unqualified as a candidate for the Presidency of the United States.

And though my research proved that Trump's character signified him to be less a man of integrity than of dishonor, less a man of genuineness than of pretense, less a man of kindness than of rudeness; nonetheless, his *professional* profile superseded all boundaries of business mores and insightful acumen. He had vision, intuition, originality, and daring, that towered him beyond customary corporate enclosed elitism. He humanized this elitism by publicly speaking his mind, and thereby, exposing his tactics, however offensively or unwisely.

Accordingly, it became clear to me that here was a man of titanic, colossal, proportions more than merely a billionaire elitist, especially since he was able to win the United States' Presidency. Could he be a mythological figure, being mightily titanic, colossal, I asked myself?

I explored that possibility satisfactorily; which, in turn, intensified my research and reflection regarding his outlandish pronouncements and extraordinary successes in entertainment, sports, properties, publishing, and all else; which seemed to justify his self-glorification. Then there was his defiance of the corporate and political status quo – all of which catapulted him into a major celebrity icon. Considering all this renown, it struck me that Trump might possibly be connected to the concept of the "übermensch" or "overman" (otherwise simply thought of as a supra-supreme man) originated by nineteenth century German philosopher, Friedrich Nietzsche. Further research on the internet showed that Nietzsche's concept of the overman had in fact been discussed in relation to Trump.

This book then took a turn toward elucidation of this possible relationship, and thus had arrived at its present purpose of proposing Trump as not related to an overman (though he seemingly shares some of the characteristic of the overman), but as a man who represents a defiance, a dismissal of outdated, inert, accepted business and political paradigms, which would seemingly lead to an <u>opening</u> of dynamic, change; thereby moving us toward what I term, *the ascendancy of justice and wisdom over injustice and ignorance*. Trump, I believe, does not represent these dynamic changes as a *person*, but they do represent him as a *supreme man of affairs* – even though both (injustice and ignorance) won him the Presidency.

It was clear to me that his supporters viewed him as their leader who would rejuvenate the political landscape of inertia and ineptitude, of stale air, to dynamic action toward America's best. America is sick; Trump will cure it – however he sees fit.

Right or wrong, time and his Presidential performance, will soon enough tell. Still, what this book can impart as to his destined role of political necessity is the following: overman or not, Trump nonetheless strides upon compulsive history with heavy boots and a wry smile through a silent, underlying all-embracing breeze that will open a little further the wisdom of our species.

This book, then, reveals the man, who through his sensational display of bluster, pretense, and the Lie, ironically furthers mankind's ever-broadening ascendancy toward authenticity, grace, justice, and wisdom. Accordingly, he will be known as an *historic necessity*.

Applying all that has been stated in this Purpose, the main theme of *Trump Manifested,* is the answer to "Who is he"? and "What is he?"

SECTION I
The Psychological Man

PART ONE

Revealed by Trump Himself

Character and Tactics Descriptions

Part One *explores the psychological character and successful tactics of Donald Trump stated in his own words, favorable to himself. These quotes indicate the distinction of the professional man and the insensitivity of the humanistic man. Both these sides of Trump won him the Presidency of the United States, and so he qualified himself as a supra-supreme man, a kind of demigod.*

[Genius]

1. There's nobody like me. Nobody.

2. I've done things that nobody else has done.

3. There is no one in my age who has accomplished more. Everyone can't be the best.

4. ["He's the great American icon".] **Trump**: "Hey, why only American? Why not the world?"

5. I am your voice. Believe me. Believe me.

6. I will save you. Only I can save you.

7. I'm the messenger, but I'll tell you what, the message is the right message.

8. I only have the power of persuasion.

9. Vision is my best asset.

10. I have amazing vision ... no one else can match.

11. I think I was born with the drive for success because I have a certain gene.

12. I rely on myself very much. I just think that you have an instinct and you go with it. Especially when it comes to deal-making and buying things.

13. I'm a strong believer in genes, that my kids can be brought up without adversity and respond well if they have the genes. I have a friend who is extraordinarily smart. But he never became successful, because he couldn't take pressure. He was buying a home and it was literally killing him – a man of forty with an I.Q. of probably a hundred and ninety. He called me one day for the umpteenth time, worrying about his mortgage and I was sitting in my chair, thinking to myself, "Here I am, buying the shuttle, the Plaza Hotel, and I don't lose an ounce of sleep over any of it. That's lucky genes."

14. I believe in hard work. I believe in being prepared and all that stuff. What in many respects, the most important thing is innate ability. ... I have it. I always had it.

15. Let me tell you, I'm a really smart guy.

16. I'm intelligent. Some people would say I'm very, very, very intelligent.

17. I know words. I have the best words.

18. There's always opposition when you do something big. I do many things that are controversial. When people see it, they love it!

19. In truth I am dazzled as much by my own creations as are the tourists and glamour hounds that flock to Trump Tower ... or any of my other properties.

20. I think apologizing is a great thing, but you have to be wrong ... I will absolutely apologize, sometime in the hopefully distant future, if I'm ever wrong.

21. I've always been able to lead; and I've led with spirit. I've just always been able to create spirit. I mean, I built a great wealth by my – *the spirit that I created* [this author's italics].

22. I was a great student. I was good at everything.

23. Not long ago I received a letter from my kindergarten teacher. It was a big surprise ... What she remembered most clearly about me is that I never stopped asking questions. I was the most inquisitive student she had ever had.

24. I have an attention span that's as long as it has to be.

25. [I have] the greatest memory in the world.

26. Even if you don't feel indomitable, act that way for a while. It helps!

27. I always go into the center.

28. I think I was born with the drive for success because I have a certain gene.

[Temperament /Character]

1. I'm honored to have the greatest temperament that anybody has.

2. I don't think people change very much. When I look at myself in the first grade and look at myself now, I am basically the same. The temperament is not that different.

3. He [his brother, Fred Jr.] totally gave of himself. And I tend to be just the opposite.

4. [his brother, Fred Jr.] was a handsome, brilliant, just the nicest guy in the world – much nicer guy than me, to be totally honest with you. I mean, the guy was great. ... Freddy just wasn't a killer ["psychological" killer].

5. I saw people really taking advantage of Fred and the lesson I learned was always to keep up my guard one hundred percent, whereas he didn't. He didn't feel that there was really reason for that, which is a fatal mistake in life.

6. People are too trusting. I'm a very untrusting guy. I study people all the time, automatically; it's my way of life, for better or worse.

7. I get bored easily; my attention span is short and probably my least favorite thing to do is to maintain the status quo. Instead of being content when everything is going fine, I start getting impatient.

8. I don't believe in crying. For whatever reason, I'm just not a crier. The closest I came was when my mother and father died. It's just not my thing. I have nothing against it when someone cries. When I see a man cry I view it as a weakness. I don't like seeing men cry.

9. [on being "a very shallow person"] That's one of my strengths. I never pretend to be anything else.

10. I'm really a nice guy. I really am.

11. I'm really not a bad person, I have to say.

12. Despite what some people may think, I'm not looking to be a bad guy when it isn't absolutely necessary.

13. I am somebody with a lot of heart.

14. I can be a killer and a nice guy. You have to be everything. You have to be strong. You have to be sweet. You have to be ruthless. And I don't think any of it can be learned. Either you have it or you don't.

15. I was thought of as like a really tough guy before the show [*The Apprentice*] and not a nice guy. Now people think I'm a tough guy, a strong guy, but sort of a nice guy.

16. I think in many cases it [the acquisition of wealth as an "absolute aphrodisiac"] really creates problems that you normally wouldn't have. … You're expected to be a certain kind of a person, and maybe you're not necessarily cut out to be that kind of a person.

17. I was a very rebellious kind of person. … I always loved to fight, all types of fights, including physical.

18. In the second grade I actually gave a teacher a black eye – I punched my music teacher because I didn't think he knew anything about music and I almost got expelled. I'm not proud of that, but it's clear evidence that even early on I had a tendency to stand up and make my opinions known in a very forceful way. The difference now is that I like to use my brain instead of my fists. [Trump note: "When I say 'punch,' when you're that age, nobody punches very hard."]

19. Growing up in Queens, I was a pretty tough kid. I wanted to be the toughest kid in the neighborhood.

20. I was a very rebellious kind of person when I was younger. I don't like to talk about it, actually. But I was a very rebellious person and very set in my ways, evidenced by the fact that I always loved to engage in any type of fight or athletic competition. In fact, I was so rebellious that my parents thought it would be a good idea for me to go to New York Military Academy for five years, starting in eighth grade.

Q: So eighth grade on?

A: Yes.

Q: Whose idea was this?

A: Well, I was very rebellious and my parents thought it would be a good idea. I was very rebellious.

Q: How did it evidence itself?

A: I loved to fight. I always loved to fight.

Q: Physical fights?

A: All types of fights. Any kind of fight, I loved it, including physical, and I was always the best athlete. Something that nobody knew about me.

21. I used to fight back all the time. My father was one tough son of a gun ("who ruled us with a steel will" – Trump). My father respects me because I stood up to him.

22. ["New York Military Academy was":] a tough, tough place. There were ex–drill sergeants all over the place. ["The instructors"] "used to beat the s- -t out of you; those guys were rough."

23. What I did basically was to convey that I respected his authority [as a baseball coach], but that he didn't intimidate me. It was a delicate balance. Like so many strong guys, [Theodore] Dobias had a tendency to go for the jugular if he smelled weakness. On other hand, if he sensed strength but you didn't try to undermine him, he treated you like a man. Fight.

24. You know what I wanted to. I wanted to hit [get even] a couple of those speakers so hard. I would have hit them. No, no. I was going to hit them, I was all set and then I got a call from a highly respected governor. ... I was gonna hit one guy in particular, a very little guy. I was gonna hit this guy so hard his head would spin and he wouldn't know what the hell happened. ... I was going to hit a number of those speakers so hard their heads would spin, they'd never recover. And that's what I did with a lot – that's why I still don't have certain people endorsing me: they still haven't recovered.

25. I love the old days, you know? You know what I hate? There's a guy totally disruptive, throwing punches, we're not allowed to punch back anymore. ... I'd like to punch him in the face, I'll tell ya. – [Donald Trump on how he would handle a protester in Nevada, sparking roaring applause from the audience, February 22, 2016]

26. There may be somebody with tomatoes in the audience. If you see somebody getting ready to throw a tomato, knock the crap out of them, would you? Seriously. Okay? Just knock the hell – I promise you, I will pay for the legal fees.

27. That was so great. Who was the person who did that? Put up your hand, put up your hand. Bring that person up here. I love that. – [Donald Trump, praising two audience members who tackled a protester at his rally in South Carolina, Feb. 16, 2016]

28. I'd rather fight than fold, because as soon as you fold once, you get the reputation of being a folder.

29. You have to fight, tooth and nail.

30. "We're all fighting battles, but I love fighting these battles."

31. Life doesn't forgive weakness.

32. I'm really good at war. I've had a lot of wars of my own. ... I love war in a certain way. But only when we win."

33. I understand the military. I know the military.

34. I could stand in the middle of Fifth Avenue and shoot somebody, and I wouldn't lose any voters, okay? It's, like, incredible.

35. [Interviewer: "You'd make a good Mafioso." – (a crime organization)]. Trump: One of the greatest.

36. I learned a long time ago that if you're not afraid to be outspoken, the media will write about you or beg you to come on their shows. So sometimes I make outrageous comments and give them what they want – viewers and readers – In order to make a point, I'm a businessman with a brand to sell.

37. I say what's on my mind kind of guy. ... If you say outrageous things and fight back, they love you. [NOTE: "In chapter two, of Trump's 2011 book *Midas Touch: Why Some Entrepreneurs Get Rich – and Why Most Don't*) he explains that he's a 'I say what's on my mind kind of guy,' but pages later explains that doesn't mean he's necessarily an honest guy."]

38. I could say whatever I wanted when I was an entrepreneur, a business guy.

39. The media loves my candor. They know I'm not going to dodge or ignore their questions. I have no problem telling it like it is.

40. I'm competitive, and I love to create challenges for myself. Maybe that's not always a good thing. It can make life complicated.

41. I am sometimes too competitive for my own good. If someone is going around labeling people winners and losers, I want to play the game and, of course, come out on the right side.

42. I believe in positive thinking, but I also believe in the power of negative thinking. You should prepare for the worst. If I'm doing a deal, I want to know how bad it's going to be if everything doesn't work rather than how good it's going to be. I have a positive outlook, but I'm unfortunately also quite cynical. So if all the negatives happened, what would my strategy be? Would I want to be in that position? If I don't, I don't do the deal. My attitude is to focus on the down side because the up side will always take care of itself. If a deal is going to be great, it's just a question of, How much am I going to make?

43. I am very skeptical about people; that's self-preservation at work. I believe that, unfortunately, people are out for themselves. At this point, it's to many people's advantage to like me. Would the phone stop ringing, would these people kissing ass disappear if things were not going well? I enjoy testing friendship.

44. I study people, and in every negotiation, I weigh how tough I should appear. I can be a killer and a nice guy. You have to be everything. You have to be strong. You have to be sweet. You have to be ruthless. And I don't think any of it can be learned. Either you have it or you don't. And that is why most kids can get straight A's in school but fail in life.

45. [Interviewer: "You seem very pleasant and charming during interviews, yet you talk constantly about toughness. Do you put on an act for us?"] I think everybody has to have some kind of filtering system [i.e., in his word: toughness]. I'm very fair and I have had the same people working for me for years. Rarely does anybody leave me.

46. I'm not tough, but I'm strong. You can't be a pussycat.

47. I've seen some real killers in my line of work, but Richard Nixon makes them look like babies. [*A Trump author*: "Donald lavishes his greatest praise on former President Nixon. ... He clearly wants his readers to believe that he is cut from the same quarry as Nixon. Indeed, his book (*Trump: Surviving at the Top*) bears more than passing similarities to Nixon's best-selling memoir, *Six Crises*."]

48. People are tired of these nice people.

[Appearances]

1. I don't want people to know exactly what I'm doing – or thinking. I like being unpredictable.

2. A very good story recently quoted a businessman describing me as "unpredictable," noting it was one of my better qualities and help me make a lot of money. Now that I am running for president, which so many experts predicted I would not do, that same trait has made it really hard for all my critics to figure out how to compete with my message. They are all busy playing nicely, following all the establishment rules, taking every predictable staff, trying to fit inside the conventional wisdom– And when I don't play that game, they don't know how to respond. ... The element of surprise wins battles. So I don't tell the other side what I'm doing, I don't warn them, and I don't let them fit me comfortably into a predictable pattern. I'll be unpredictable. It keeps them off balance.

3. It's always good to be underestimated.

4. I can sit down with the most sophisticated. People in the arts in New York and get along fabulously with them. If I want to, I can convince them that I know is much about something as they do, and I don't. [Asked how he manages this trick, Trump said,] It's a feeling, and an aura that you create.

5. When you start studying yourself too deeply, you start seeing things that maybe you don't want to see. And if there's a rhyme and reason, people can figure you out, and once they can figure you out, you're in big trouble.

6. It's always good to do things nice and complicated so that nobody can figure it out.

7. I'm the Ernest Hemingway of 140 characters.

[Ego]

1. Nothing wrong with ego. People need ego.

2. I've never once in my life known a person who was successful who didn't have a big ego. Ego's not a bad thing.

3. Show me someone without an ego, and I'll show you a loser.

4. I don't like losers.

5. I have a wealthy friend who called me up to see if I could get him reservations at Jean-Georges Restaurant and I had to ask myself, "What's the point of his immense success if he can't even get a reservation?" No one has ever heard about him – he's shy about using his name. He has to call other people, like me, to help him out. That got me thinking about the toot-your-own-horn theory, which is something I believe in. This poor rich guy is a

perfect example of why I believe in it. The power of a name can be incredible. It can open doors like nothing else.

Until you have a "household name" you might do well to tell people who you are and what you've done. It's a start. It's also a way of networking to find out if you might have common interests.

6. I'm the king of Palm Beach ... [Celebrities and rich people] all come over. They all eat, they all love me, they all kiss my ass. And then they all leave and say, 'Isn't he horrible.' But I'm the king.

7. I think you have to have – you know, I don't consider myself to have a big ego. The fact is, I have never, however, met a person who's successful who didn't have an ego or a fairly substantial – there's nothing wrong with having an ego. ... I don't even express it [his ego]. I mean, I put my name on buildings because it sells better. I don't do it because, gee, I need that. I mean, I get more per square foot in New York than anybody else by far. I get – If you build a building here, and I build a building there, and not to use you, but I will get substantially more per square foot in that building than the person building the building across the street for almost the same building.

8. I satisfy myself.

9. Having an ego and acknowledging it is a healthy choice. Think about it: If you can't say great things about yourself, who do you think will? So don't be afraid to toot your own horn when you've done something worth tooting about.

10. Every successful person has a very large ego. [Interviewer: "Every successful person? Mother Teresa? Jesus Christ?"] Far greater egos than you will ever understand.

[Vanity]

1. Vanity? Sure. Maybe it [his hairstyle] is, maybe it isn't. I don't know, I don't think of it.

2. Look at those hands, are they small hands? And, [Republican rival Marco Rubio] referred to my hands: 'If they're small, something else must be small.' I guarantee you there's no problem. I guarantee.

3. My fingers are long and beautiful, as, it has been well documented, [as] are various other parts of my body.

4. Good looks have been my top – and sometimes, to be honest, my only – priority in my man-about-town days.

5. It's very hard for them to attack me on looks, because I'm so good looking.

6. One thing about television, it brings out personality. People are able to

watch me in action. They hear my voice and see my eyes. There's nothing I can hide. That's me. Television brings out your flaws, your weaknesses, your strengths, and your truths. The audience either likes you or it doesn't.

7. I think maybe one of my greatest strengths is understanding people, you know, specific people for specific jobs, and just understanding the human psyche of other people, maybe not even my own quite as well, but of other people. And I'd like to think that I can tell the difference between somebody that's looking for one thing and somebody that's looking for the other. ... But you really never can, I mean, no matter how well you understand people until there's a time of test, and we shall see what we shall see.

8. [at one time in his high-rolling career] I got a little cocky and, probably, a little bit lazy. I wasn't working as hard, and I wasn't focusing on the basics. I traveled around the world to the spring fashion shows in France.

9. I began to socialize more, probably too much. Frankly, I was bored. I really felt I could do no wrong. Sort of like a baseball player who keeps hitting home runs or a golfer who keeps winning tournaments – you just get a feeling of invincibility. Ultimately, this invincible feeling, while positive at times, can be destructive. You let down your guard. You don't work as hard. Then things start to go in the wrong direction. And that's what happened to me – and I never thought it could. In 1990, the market was so horrendous that prices, for even the best buildings in town, were plummeting. Apartments were being bought at prices you never thought possible. It was a complete disaster.

[Revenge]

1. I believe that, unfortunately, people are out for themselves.

2. I love getting even when I get screwed by someone.

3. My motto is: Always get even. When somebody screws you, screw them back in spades.

4. When someone attacks me, I attack back. Hard.

5.. When I'm wounded, I go after people hard. I try and unwound myself

6. I can't stomach disloyalty ... and now I go out of my way to make her life miserable.

7. When somebody tries to sucker-punch me, when they're after my ass, I push back a hell of a lot harder than I was pushed in the first place. If somebody tries to push me around, he's going to pay a price. Those people don't come back for seconds. I don't like being pushed around or taken advantage of.

8. For many years I've said that if someone screws you, screw them back. When somebody hurts you, just go after them as viciously and as violently as you can.

9. As bad as things got for me – and they got pretty bad – I never let anyone push me around. This saved my ass. I always sent out the message: "Don't lie to me. Don't cheat me. Because I'll find out and I'll find you and it won't be pretty."

10. I really value my reputation and I don't hesitate to sue.

11. I'm a guy who lies awake at night and thinks and plots.

[Showmanship]

1. Controversy, in short, sells.

2. Interviewer: "Then what does all this – the yacht, the bronze tower, the casinos – really mean to you?" Props for the show.

3. The show is 'Trump.' And it is sold-out performances everywhere.

4. [Interviewer: "So building that second huge yacht isn't an act of gaudy excess but another act in the show?"] Well, it draws people. It will be the eighth wonder of the world and will create an aura that seems to work. It will cost me two hundred million dollars. But I don't need it! I could be very happy living in a one-bedroom apartment. I used to live that life. In the early Seventies, I lived in a studio apartment overlooking a water tank.

5. There are two publics as far as I'm concerned. The real public and then there's the New York society horseshit. The real public has always liked Donald Trump. The real public feels that Donald Trump is going through Trump-bashing. When I go out now, forget about it. I'm mobbed. It's bedlam.

6. My attitude is if somebody's willing to pay me $225,000 to make a speech, it seems stupid not to show up. You know why I'll do it? Because I don't think anyone's ever been paid that much.

7. If you don't tell people about your success, they probably won't know about it.

8. I know how to sell. Selling is life. You can have the greatest singer in the world, but if nobody knows who he is, he'll never have the opportunity to sing.

9. There are singers in the world with voices as good as Frank Sinatra's, but they're singing in their garages because no one has ever heard of them. You need to generate interest, and you need to create excitement."

10. Because I've been successful, make money, get headlines, and have authored bestselling books, I have a better chance to make my ideas public than do people who are less well known.

[Emotions]

1. [As regards] my own feelings, as to where the world is, where the world is going, and that can change rapidly from day to day. Then you have a September 11th, and you don't feel so good about yourself and you don't feel so good about the world and you don't feel so good about New York City. Then you have a year later, and the city is as hot as a pistol. Even months after that it was a different feeling. So yeah, even my own feelings affect my value to myself.

2. You can't be emotional in business; it can flat out kill you.

3. I use emotion for the many, and use reason for the few.

[Conflict]

1. I *do* believe in hate when it's appropriate.

2. Unite to win. Divide to conquer.

3. Rules are meant to be broken.

4. For the most part, you can't respect people because most people aren't worthy of respect.

5. Sometimes you need conflict in order to come up with a solution, settlement; so I'm aggressive, but I also get things done, and in the end, everybody likes me.

6. You've got to have these guys [his two bodyguards]. . . . You know, these guys get a little carried away sometimes, but they're basically good guys. . . but they need that, Jack. It's good for their minds to rough people up a little. Sometimes you have to give up the fight and walk away, and move on to something that's more productive.

7. I became very popular after I started firing people every week [on his TV show, "The Apprentice"].

[Toughness]

1. I have a reputation of being tough, and I'd like to think it's justified. You *must* be tough when a lot of influential people are saying that your day has come and gone, when your marriage is breaking up, and when business pressures are increasing. Toughness, in the long run, is major secret of my survival.

2. Toughness, as I see it, is a quality of equal parts of strength, intelligence, and self-respect. I think I became intrigued with the quality as I grew up and watched what was happening to my older brother, Fred, a great and talented guy who had a career as an airline pilot but who died of alcoholism a few years

ago. Fred, though I loved him dearly, was not traditionally tough. He was sweet and trusting, and as a result, people constantly took advantage of him. Watching what happened to Fred, I learned to study people closely and always to keep my guard up, in both my personal and my professional life. Fred was truly one of my great teachers.

3. Occasionally, yes, toughness *does* involve some old-fashioned ass-kicking.

4. Despite what many people think, being tough has nothing to do with bullying people. A bully to me is someone who is trying to work out some psychological problem by intimidating people. The real estate business, especially in New York, is full of bullies – people who've gotten somewhere in the past by screaming at their adversaries, their employees, their spouses. _____ is a bully who is driven mostly by a desire to intimidate others or to get away with something that other people can't. Being a good businesswoman is, to her, secondary to being a bitch on wheels.

5. Usually, I'm friendly, polite, and upbeat in my dealings with my employees and even with business adversaries. I don't recommend speaking sternly to people or throwing your weight around unless it serves some clear purpose.

6. The opposite of toughness – weakness – makes me mad and sometimes turns my stomach. I'm not referring here to the kind of weakness that comes from being poor, sick, or disadvantaged. I'm talking about those people who can take a strong stand but just don't. That's why I've started to speak out about what is happening to America, particularly on the business front.

7. The fact is that there is a certain logic in the professionals' reluctance to take a stand. Toughness is scary. … When we fear leaders of great passion, though, what we often forget is that the other side fears them too. I remember reading that Hitler, as he rose to power during his early years, continually talked to the people around him about Winston Churchill. "Keep an eye on that man," he kept saying. "He's going to be one of our biggest problems." The English politicians criticized Churchill for calling Hitler a mad dog; it wasn't diplomatic – in fact, they said, it was downright inflammatory. Yet Hitler, in his way, respected Churchill, whom he recognized as not just a government official but rather an advocate for the English people – a man who would never stop pushing and pressuring until he got what he wanted. And Hitler was right about that, of course. When Hitler's people told him that Churchill was politically dead, no longer a problem, Hitler stated that Churchill would re-emerge – "People like that never die."

8. One of our biggest problems today is that we have too few advocates. What we have instead are too many weaklings and compromisers.

9. For a nation, toughness means avoiding complacency, meeting and solving problems head-on, and be willing to use power for goals you know are honorable.

10. In business, toughness means playing by the rules but also putting those rules to work for you. It is looking at an adversary across the desk and saying simply, No.

11. Sometimes, if you hang in there long enough and, as the boxing trainers always say, "Keep punching till the bell," people take notice and give you a boost.

12. As I've said repeatedly in my first book and in this one, I believe in working hard. I believe in being smart and not cute. I don't respect cheaters. My admiration is reserved for those who have achieved greatness and then topped themselves.

13. I'm never satisfied – which is my way of saying that there is a great deal I still want to do and believe I should do.

14. Some people are always saying that I can't go on like this forever, and that I'm at the beginning of the end. I'd rather see myself as being at the end of the beginning.

15. [Interviewer: "You seem very pleasant and charming during interviews, yet you talk constantly about toughness. Do you put on an act for us?"] I think everybody has to have some kind of filtering system [i.e. toughness]. I'm very fair and I have had the same people working for me for years. Rarely does anybody leave me. But when somebody tries to sucker-punch me, when they're after my ass, I push back a hell of a lot harder than I was pushed in the first place. If somebody tries to push me around, he's going to pay a price. Those people don't come back for seconds. I don't like being pushed around or taken advantage of.

16. I admire toughness in people.

17. Sometimes you have to give up the fight and walk away, and move on to something that's more productive.

18. I want to hate these muggers and murderers. They should be forced to suffer and when they kill they should be executed for their crimes.

19. So, in the end, what is toughness, as I see it, midway through my life? Toughness is pride, drive, commitment, and the courage to follow through on things you believe in, even when they are under attack. It is solving problems instead of letting them fester. It is being who you really are, even when society wants you to be someone else. Toughness is walking away from things you want because, for one reason or another, acquiring them doesn't make sense.

Toughness is knowing how to be a gracious winner – and rebounding quickly when you lose.

[Racism]

1. I don't have a racist bone in my body.

2. I am the least racist person there is. And I think most people that know me would tell you that. I am the least racist.

3. I have a great relationship with the blacks. I've always had a great relationship with the blacks.

4. I've got to tell you something else. I think that the guy is lazy. Probably not his fault because this is a trait in Blacks. It really is, I believe that. ... Don't you agree? ... [in response to the remark that that kind of remark could be damaging to his image:] Yeah, you're right, If anybody ever heard me say that ... Holy s_ _t ... I'd be in a lot of trouble. But I have to tell you, that's the way I feel. ... It's a trait.

5. Black guys counting my money! I hate it. The only kind of people I want counting my money are little short guys that wear yarmulkes every day.

6. I grew up in New York City, a town with different races, religions, and peoples. It breeds tolerance. In all truth, I don't care whether or not a person is gay. I judge people based on their capability, honesty, and merit. Being in the entertainment business – that is, owning casinos and ... several large beauty pageants – I've worked with many gay people. I have met some tough, talented, capable, terrific people. Their lifestyle is of no interest to me. ... When you hang with people who are different from you, you get an appreciation for other cultures.

[Women]

1. I don't know why, but I seem to bring out either the best or worst in women.

2. I've been told I'm a role model to many women.

3. I respect women incredibly. I have had women working for me in positions that they've never worked in terms of construction, in terms of so many different jobs. I had a woman who was in charge of the building of Trump Tower, many years ago, before anybody would have even thought of it, and did a fantastic job. I have given women more opportunity than I would say virtually anybody in the construction industry.

4. I have women working in high positions. I was one of the first people to put women in charge of big construction jobs. And, you know, I've had a great relationship with women.

5. They [women] do want to be taken care of and they do want to be cherished and they do want to be respected.

6. I cherish women. I want to help women. I'm going to be able to do things for women that no other candidate would be able to do.

7. I believe strongly in the concept of 'the woman behind the man,' or vice versa.

8. I have a daughter named Ivanka and a wife named Melania who constantly want me to talk about women's health issues because they know how I feel about it and they know how I feel about women. I respect women, I love women, I cherish women. You know, Hillary Clinton said, "He shouldn't cherish," well I said, I do cherish, I love women. ... I will take care of women, and I have great respect for women. I do cherish women. And I will take care of women.

9. I have tremendous respect for women, and I am going to protect women. . . . (My daughter Ivanka) said, "Dad, you respect and love women so much, could you talk about it more because people don't really understand how you feel."

10. There's nothing I love more than women, but they're really a lot different than portrayed. They are far worse than men, far more aggressive; and boy, can they be smart. Let's give credit where credit is due, and let's salute women for their tremendous power, which most men are afraid to admit they have.

11. Women have one of the great acts of all time. The smart ones act very feminine and needy, but inside they are real killers. The person who came up with the expression 'the weaker sex' was either very naive or had to be kidding. I have seen women manipulate men with just a twitch of their eye – or perhaps another body part.

12. Beauty and elegance, whether in a woman, a building, or a work of art, is not just superficial or something pretty to see.

13. My favorite part [of the movie, *Pulp Fiction*] is when Sam has his gun out in the diner and he tells the guy to tell his girlfriend to shut up. "Tell that bitch to be cool. Say: 'Bitch be cool.'" I love those lines.

14. [Asked if he treats women with respect] I can't say that.

15. Women, you have to treat them like s- - t.

16. I tell friends who treat their wives magnificently, get treated like crap in return, 'Be rougher and you'll see a different relationship.'

17. I grew up in a very normal family. I was always of the opinion that aggression, sex drive, and everything that goes along with it was on the man's

part of the table, not the woman's. As I grew older and witnessed life firsthand from a front-row seat at the great clubs, social events, and parties of the world – I have seen just about everything – I began to realize that women are far stronger than men. Their sex drive makes us look like babies. Some women try to portray themselves as being of the weaker sex, but don't believe it for a minute.

18. I knew a guy named Ben who was very worldly-wise. Ben, I was sure, could serve as this woman's escort and be discreet about it. ... She turned out to be the wife of a man who was then the prime minister of a major country. I'd heard stories about this lady, but I never thought much of them until that night. We met at the house of the friend who'd phoned me. After we'd all chatted for a while in the living room, the four of us who already knew each other drifted out to the kitchen, leaving Ben and Madame X in the living room to get better acquainted. Which they did. In fact, when we drifted back in, about ten minutes later, she and Ben were involved in an incredibly torrid scene on the couch. I remember standing there and thinking to myself, "Well, Donald, you're not in Queens anymore."

19. I think any man enjoys flirtations, and if he said he didn't, he'd be lying or he'd be a politician trying to get the extra four votes. I think everybody likes knowing he's well responded to. Especially as you get into certain strata where there is an ego involved and a high level of success, it's important. People really like the idea that other people respond well to them.

20. My favorite part [of the movie, *Pulp Fiction*] is when Sam has his gun out in the diner and he tells the guy to tell his girlfriend to shut up. "Tell that bitch to be cool. Say: 'Bitch be cool.'" I love those lines.

21. I was especially carefree [in the early-mid 1970s]. I had a comfortable little studio apartment in Third Avenue in the city, and I maintained a lifestyle that was fairly commonplace then but that now, in an age when people are worried about dying from sex, is hard to even imagine. I didn't drink or take drugs; as far as stimulants go, I've yet to have my first cup of coffee. But I was out four or five nights a week, usually with a different woman each time, and I was enjoying myself immensely.

22. I've never had any trouble in bed, but if I'd had affairs with half the starlets and female athletes the newspapers linked me with, I'd have no time to breathe.

23. [On men having threesomes] "Haven't we all? Are we babies?"

24. [On how he's 'banged some of the greatest beauties on the planet,' according to Howard Stern] "That is true. Some of the greats in history."

25. You really want to know what I consider ideal company? A total piece of ass.

26. I have really given a lot of women great opportunity. Unfortunately, after they are a star, the fun is over for me.

27. Well, I'll tell you the funniest is that before a show [his Beauty Pageant], I'll go backstage, and everyone's getting dressed, and everything else, and you know, no men are anywhere, and I'm allowed to go in because I'm the owner of the pageant; and therefore, I'm inspecting it. You know, I'm inspecting because I want to make sure that everything is good. ... Is everyone OK? You know, they're standing there with no clothes. And you see these incredible looking women. And, so, I sort of get away with things like that.

28. All of the women on The Apprentice flirted with me – consciously or unconsciously. That's to be expected.

29. A sexual dynamic is always present between people, unless you are asexual.

30. You know, it really doesn't matter what (the media) write as long as you've got a young and beautiful piece of ass."

31. [Interviewer: What is it at 35? It's called check-out time.] "No, I have no age—I mean, 150. I have an age limit. I don't want to be like _____, with, you know, 12-year-olds."

32. [Told interviewer that he'd have "no problem" sleeping with 24-year-olds.]

33. [Interviewer: "Would you have a black woman in bed?" he responded:] "Well, it depends on what your definition of black is."

34. Referred to his bed as 'The rainbow coalition', "as _____ would say."

35. [To the founder of "Playboy" magazine:] "It's hard for me to tell which of these girls are yours, and which ones are mine."

36. I mean, the women, some of the women, happen to be very attractive. And they have used their sexuality to win certain tasks, as we call them. And hey, that's part of life, I guess. In real life, that happens, too. I've known it. I've seen it happen.

37. I mean, some incredible, beautiful women, they'll walk up, and they'll flip their top, and they'll flip their panties.

38. They wear thongs, they wear bikinis, they wear high heels. They wear just about everything that you're not supposed to wear because that's not politically correct.

39. "Said he (Donald Trump) *should be getting the Congressional Medal of Honor* after the interviewer said he's braver than any Vietnam vet because [he's] *out there screwing a lot of women."*

40. Don't you think my daughter's hot? She's hot, right?

41. Said to 14-year-old girls: "Wow! Just think—in a couple of years I'll be dating you."

42. Some women are highly aggressive and they want sex, no different from men and sometimes worse.

43. Told a radio host that it was OK to call his daughter Ivanka "a piece of ass."

44. You know, it really doesn't matter what they write [the media], as long as you've got a young and beautiful piece of ass; ... but, she's got to be young and beautiful.

45. [On approaching women:] Move forward. Even if you get smacked.

46. I remember attending a magnificent dinner being given by one of the most admired people in the world. I was seated next to a lady of great social pedigree and wealth. Her husband was sitting on the other side of the table, and we were having a very nice but extremely straight conversation. All of a sudden I felt her hand on my knee, then on my leg. She started petting me in all different ways. I looked at her and asked, "Is everything all right?" I didn't want to make a scene in a ballroom full of five hundred VIPs. The amazing part about her was who she was – one of the biggest of the big. She then asked me to dance, and I accepted. While we were dancing she became very aggressive, and I said, "We have a problem. Your husband is sitting at the table, and so is my wife."

"Donald", she said. "I don't care. I just don't care. I have to have you, and I have to have you now." I told her that I'd call her, but that she had to stop the behavior immediately. She made me promise, and I did. When I called I just called to say hello, and that was the end of that. But the level of aggression was unbelievable. This is not infrequent, it happens all the time.

47. They're [deeply troubled women] always the best in bed. ... It's just unbelievable. You don't want to be with them for long term, but for the short term there's nothing like it.

48. If I told the real stories of my experiences with women, often seemingly very happily married and important women, this book would be a guaranteed best-seller (which it will be anyway). I'd love to tell all, using names and places, but I just don't think it's right.

49. You know, I'm automatically attracted to beautiful – I just start kissing them. It's like a magnet. Just kiss. I don't even wait. And when you're a star, they let you do it. You can do anything.

50. Oftentimes when I was sleeping with one of the top women in the world I would say to myself, thinking about me as a boy from Queens, "Can you believe what I am getting?"

51. I did try and f- -k her. She was married. I moved on her very heavily. In fact, I took her out furniture shopping. She wanted to get some furniture. I said, I'll show you where they have some nice furniture. I moved on her like a bitch, but I couldn't get there and she was married. Then all of a sudden I see her, she's now got the big phony tits and everything. I'm automatically attracted to beautiful – I just start kissing them. It's like a magnet. Just kiss. I don't even wait. When you're a star, they let you do it. You can do anything. Grab 'em by the p- - -y. You can do anything.

52. I think that, nowadays, a lot of things have changed, just changed so drastically over the last years [regarding a politician's personal sexual affairs life in seeking the high office or being in high office]. I mean, Gary Hart, in all fairness, somebody was sitting on his lap, and he was run out of office like a dog. And, then, you go through the whole Clinton thing, and it's like, this is major league stuff. ... I think that, nowadays, a lot of things have changed, just changed so drastically over the last years. ... I don't think it matters at all. You know, I have some really fantastic – I've had over the years some really fantastic relationships and with some really spectacular women and wonderful women and nice women. And, you know, I don't think it matters, but, you know, you never know what happens.

53. Witness the difference between the two women [his wives] who have meant the most to me in my life to date, Ivana and Marla. Both are incredibly talented and successful women in their own right. In short, they're both blond and beautiful. The impact they've had on me is profound.

54. Marriage is a very important thing for people. I fully believe it. I think that having the home and having the stability, and I've had it all different ways. I mean, I've had it the other way, and I've had it the marriage way, and I think that marriage is very important. Having a good wife and having a nice family is very, very important. There is no substitute for it, frankly. There really is no substitute for it. I think it's [friendship with your marriage partner] the most important thing. I mean you have to be best friends. If you're not going to be best friends, then the marriage cannot work. No matter what the other ingredients are, the marriage really can't work.

55. A good marriage is like negotiating an important deal: You have to consider all the factors, thoughtfully and thoroughly. If you were investing a large part of yourself and your fortune into a venture, believe me, you'd make sure you thought about it for a long time first. That's how I see marriage. It's serious, and it's important. I don't approach it any more haphazardly than I do a very important deal. In fact, considering the amount of deals I've made compared to the number of marriages I've had, I'd say I'm quite cautious about marriage.

56. For a man to be successful he needs support at home, just like my father had from my mother, not someone who is always griping and bitching. When a man has to endure a woman who is not supportive and complains constantly about his not being home enough or not being attentive enough, he will not be very successful unless he is unable to cut the cord.

57. I knew from the start that Ivana was different from just about all of the other women I'd been spending time with. Good looks had been my top – and sometimes, to be honest, my only – priority in my man-about-town days. Ivana was gorgeous, but she was also ambitious and intelligent. When I introduced her to friends and associates, I said, "Believe me. This one's different." Everyone knew what I meant, and I think everyone sensed that I found the combination of beauty and brains almost unbelievable. I suppose I was a little naive, and perhaps, like a lot of men, I had been taught by Hollywood that one woman couldn't have both.

58. My marriage, it seemed, was the only area of my life in which I was willing to accept something less than perfection. ... I grew up with the American Dream of sharing life with a wife and children, and that's not something you just toss aside easily. I also stayed with Ivana because, as in most marriages, there was pressure to keep things intact. ... There's nothing wrong, of course, with worrying about the effects of divorce on your children and the other people around you. The problem is that those considerations aren't enough to keep a marriage together. You can go for counseling, you can have heart-to-heart talks, you can stay together 'for the sake of the kids.' But, in the end, it's always better for everyone if some couples part.

59. I even thought, briefly, about approaching Ivana with the idea of an 'open marriage.' But I realized there was something hypocritical and tawdry about such an arrangement that neither of us could live with – especially Ivana. She's too much of a lady.

60. My big mistake with Ivana was taking her out of the role of wife and allowing her to run one of my casinos in Atlantic City, then the Plaza Hotel. The problem was, work was all she wanted to talk about. When I got home at night, rather than talking about the softer subjects of life, she wanted to tell me how

well the Plaza was doing, or what a great day the casino had. I really appreciated all her efforts, but it was just too much. ... I will never again give a wife responsibility within my business. Ivana worked very hard, and I appreciated the effort, but I soon began to realize that I was married to a businessperson rather than a wife.

61. I would never buy Ivana any decent jewels or pictures. Why give her negotiable assets?

62. [Regarding Ivana's belief that Donald had engaged in extramarital relations, to which he replied:] Continuing love and affection was not a material part of the 1987 [pre-nuptial] agreement.

63. [Donald allows that he is at least somewhat to blame for causing a public scandal over the breakup of his marriage to Ivana.] Ultimately, I have to confess, the way I handled the situation was a copout. I never sat down calmly with Ivana to 'talk it out.' As I probably should have.

64. [Regarding Marla, wife No. 2] I was bored when she was walking down the aisle. I kept thinking: What the hell am I doing here? I was so deep into my business stuff. I couldn't think of anything else.

65. For me, business comes easier than relationships.

66. I'm married to my business. It's been a marriage of love. So, for a woman, frankly, it's not easy in terms of relationships. But there are a lot of assets.

67. I don't have very much time [for intimate relationships]. I just don't have very much time. There's nothing I can do about what I do other than stopping. And I just don't want to stop.

68. My marriage to Marla lasted three and a half years. Sadly, like so many couples these days, we drifted apart. Our lifestyles became less and less compatible. We wanted different things. Marla was content when it was just her, [their daughter] Tiffany, and me. I, on the other hand, realized that business needed to be taken care of constantly. When two people have such a difference in opinion regarding the lifestyle they want to lead, there is no longer any reason to stay together.

69. Marla was always wanting me to spend more time with her. 'Why can't you be home at five o'clock like other husbands?' she would ask. Sometimes, when I was in the wrong mood, I would give a very materialistic answer. 'Look, I like working. You don't mind traveling around in beautiful helicopters and airplanes, and you don't mind living at the top of Trump Tower, or at Mar-a-Lago, or traveling to the best hotels, or shopping in the best stores and never having to worry about money, do you? If you want me to be home at five o'clock, maybe these other things wouldn't happen and you'd be complaining

about that, too. Why would you want to take something that I enjoy and change it?' I always viewed her whys as being very selfish. But the fact is, in a marriage both sides have to be happy.

70. Often, I will tell friends whose wives are constantly nagging them about this or that that they're better off leaving and cutting their losses. I'm not a great believer in always trying to work things out, because it just doesn't happen that way. For a man to be successful he needs support at home, just like my father had from my mother, not someone who is always griping and bitching. When a man has to endure a woman who is not supportive and complains constantly about his not being home enough or not being attentive enough, he will not be very successful unless he is able to cut the cord.

71. I don't want to have to go home and have to work at a relationship. A relationship you have to work at, in my opinion doesn't work.

72. You need love, you need trust, you need sex, you need lots of different things – all of which are very complex.

73. You know, I don't want to sound too much like a chauvinist, but when I come home and dinner's not ready, I'll go through the roof, okay?

74. Pregnancy is ... a wonderful thing for the woman. It's a wonderful thing for the husband. It's certainly an inconvenience for a business.

75. I think that putting a wife to work is a very dangerous thing.

76. [He] Called a female attorney *disgusting* because she had to pump breast milk.

77. [He] "Said derogatory comments he made about women were for *the purpose of entertainment.*"

78. [He] "Said a New York Times columnist has *the face of a dog!*"

79. I promise not to talk about your plastic surgery that didn't work.

80. [She] is disgusting, both inside and out. If you take a look at her, she's a slob. How does she even get on television?

81. [She] has the brains of someone who was born yesterday and the body of someone who died last week.

82. Look at that face! Would anyone vote for that? Can you imagine that, the face of our next president?! I mean, [she's] a woman, and I'm not supposed to say bad things, but really, folks, come on. Are we serious?

83. You could see there was blood coming out of [her] eyes; blood coming out of her whatever.

84. [Said his ex-wife's accent:] got worse as she grew older and It was like the

Chinese torture. You know, the water drops on your head.

85. Women usually will put their families first, or at least give them equal time. The families win, but often that's why women perceive a glass ceiling looming overhead.

86. There are basically three types of women and reactions. One is the good woman who very much loves her future husband, solely for himself, but refuses to sign the agreement on principle. I fully understand this, but the man should take a pass anyway and find someone else. The other is the calculating woman who refuses to sign the prenuptial agreement because she is expecting to take advantage of the poor, unsuspecting sucker she's got in her grasp. There is also the woman who will openly and quickly sign a prenuptial agreement in order to make a quick hit and take the money given to her.

87. The most difficult aspect of the prenuptial agreement is informing your future wife (or husband): I love you very much, but just in case things don't work out, this is what you will get in the divorce.

88. I was proud of myself. I reprimanded the women [candidates on *The Apprentice*] not to rely on short skirts and cleavage ... kisses and phone numbers. ... Can you imagine me, of all people, reprimanding the women for using too much sex? I was very proud of myself.

[Children]
1. Truthfully, I was a much better father than a husband. I was always working too much to be the husband my wives wanted me to be. I blame myself. I was making my marketing real estate and business and it was very hard for a relationship to compete with that aspect of my life.

2. [What children mean to him] A lot ... You've got to have them, man. You know, it keeps you going. I have good kids, so it makes it a little easier. It keeps the whole wheel going.

3. The ultimate definition [of a good father] is somebody whose children really love them ... If the kids loved the parents, that's on the way to being a good definition.

4. I continue to stay young, right? I produce children, I stay young.

5. Now I know Melania; I'm not gonna to be doing the diapers, I'm not gonna be making the food, I may never even see the kids. She'll be an unbelievable mother. I'll be a good father.

6. I'll tell you what I've learned: Children are tough. Much tougher than people think. ... I'm a really good father, but not a really good husband. You've probably figured out my children really like me – love me – a lot. It's hard when

somebody walks into the living room of Mar-a-Lago in Palm Beach and this is supposed to be, like, a normal life. But they're very grounded and very solid.

7. The hardest thing for me about raising kids has been finding the time. I know friends who leave their business so they can spend more time with their children, and I say, 'Gimme a break!' My children could not love me more if I spent fifteen times more time with them.

[Honesty]

1. I see myself as a very honest guy stationed in a very corrupt world.

2. I think I'm so honest that it gets me in trouble. I'm a very smart person, I could give an answer that's perfect; and everything is fine and nobody would care about it, nobody would write about it; or I could give an honest answer, which becomes a big story. I think it will help me. I think people are tired of politically correct people where everything comes out "The sun will rise and be beautiful." I think people are really tired of politically correct. I just attacked the Central Part Five Settlement. Who's going to do that? You know what you have to do? You have to fight, tooth and nail.

3. You must be honest with yourself.

[Friendship]

1. I would say that I have a lot of very good friends. But again, my business is so all encompassing I don't really get the pleasure of being with friends that much frankly.

2. To me, friendship can be really tested only in bad times.

3. I enjoy testing friendships.

4. [He explained his political hopscotching as pure pragmatism.] It had to do more with practicality; because if you're going to run for office, you would have had to make friends.

5. [From praising his political opponents to insulting them] I was a business-man, and I had to get along with everybody. Now I'm a politician, I guess. But when I'm a businessman I get along with everybody.

6. You know the funny thing, I don't get along with rich people. I get along with the middle class and the poor people better than I get along with the rich people.

[Beauty]

1. Everyone knows how important beauty is to me. I always try to have it in my life. I hire the best people, find the most fabulous locations, and use the finest materials to make sure that every project I undertake is truly

exceptional. Being surrounded by beauty makes me feel great; it enhances every part of my life, and I deserve it.

2. Beauty and elegance, whether in a woman, a building, or a work of art, is not just superficial or something pretty to see. Beauty and elegance are products of personal style that come from deep within.

3. My style is based on trying to make whatever I do breathtakingly beautiful. People react emotionally to my style; they want more of it. It's no accident that I'm so involved with beauty; it's my signature, my brand, and I think it's best to have it in spades.

4. Contact with beauty exposes successful people to an excellence from which they can learn, grow, and improve their lives. Beauty rewards people for all their hard work.

5. I love to take an undeveloped piece of property and turn it into something magnificent.

6. I don't do it for the money. I've got enough, much more than I'll ever need. I do it to do it. Deals are my art form. Others paint beautifully on canvas or write wonderful poetry. I like making deals, preferably big deals. That's how I get my kicks.

7. I look at things for the art sake and the beauty sake and for the deal sake.

[Reading]
1. When I say I read a lot, I'm talking about current reading of the press and the media. I would love to read.

2. I never have [had time to read]. I'm always busy doing a lot. Now I'm more busy, I guess, than ever before.

3. [He said in a series of interviews that he does not need to read extensively because he reaches the right decisions] ... with very little knowledge other than the knowledge I [already] had, plus the words 'common sense,' because I have a lot of common sense and I have a lot of business ability.

4. I like to read Greek philosophers.

5. I read books – usually biographies.

6. I'm one of those people who don't require a lot of sleep – maybe three or four hours a night. So, what do I do with those extra hours? I read.

7. I read as much as I can, but not as much as I'd like.

[Learning]
1. If I'd started in business thinking I knew everything, I'd have been sunk before I started. Never think of learning as being a burden or studying as being

boring. It may require some discipline, but it can be an adventure. It can also prepare you for a new beginning.

2. I'm highly educated, which, until *The Apprentice* [his exceptionally popular TV show] most people didn't know. They thought I was a barbarian. But I'm highly educated.

3. The more you learn, the more you realize how much you don't know. Learning in itself is an investment.

[Stimulants]

1. I have never had a drug in my life.

2. I've never had a cigarette, I've never had a glass of alcohol.

3. People think I am a gambler. I've never gambled in my life.

[Humility]

1. If you want to know if I've ever been wrong, the best thing to do would be to ask my kids. They'll tell you the truth about that.

2. Of course I've done things wrong. Show me a human being who hasn't. But when I do, I go out and try to make things right. I tried to do a better job going forward.

3. Ten years ago, bad publicity was much harder for me to take than it is now. It is almost irrelevant.

4. It used to bug the hell out of me when I'd drop out of the bidding for something and then get a call from a reporter asking, 'So Mr. Trump, how does it feel to get beat?'

5. A little more moderation would be good. Of course, my life hasn't exactly been one of moderation.

6. I'm more humble than people might think.

7. I think I am actually humble. I think I'm much more humble than you would understand.

[Altruism]

1. It's [his feeling of guilt about his wealth] not overriding, but I do have it. ... I do have a feeling of guilt. I'm living well and like it, I know that many other people don't live particularly well. I do have a social consciousness. I'm setting up a foundation; I give a lot of money away and I think people respect that. The fact that I built this large company by myself, working people respect that; but the people who are at high levels don't like it. They'd like it for themselves.

2. I give to everybody. When they call, I give. And do you know what? When I need something from them two years later, three years later, I call them, they

are there for me.

3. I have done a couple of things which maybe on the outside don't appear to be very humanitarian but I think inwardly I think they probably are [reasons why he's here on earth for a purpose]. We have created thousands of jobs for people that maybe wouldn't have jobs today. We've created, you know, industry in the city which again while today it's thriving and probably considered the best five years ago. At the time we did it, it was not considered to be thriving, and in my own way I suspect that we've just created a certain amount of happiness in many houses where instead of going on a welfare line or whatever the people have now come home with a nice paycheck, who are now working successfully in one of our developments. So, I think in a sense maybe I was put on earth to help fulfill that function, and I think that's an important function.

[Success]

1. I have great respect for people who have found their success the hard way.

2. Success requires work seven days per week.

3. A simple formula for success: Deliver the goods.

4. Success breeds success.

5. Most people think small, because most people are afraid of success, afraid of making decisions, afraid of winning … that gives people like me a great advantage.

6. To be successful you have to separate yourself from 98 percent of the rest of the world.

7. Most successful people have very short attention spans. It has a lot to do with imagination.

8. You have to be as tough as nails and willing to kick ass if you want to win.

9. Having an ego and acknowledging it is a healthy choice. Think about it: If you can't say great things about yourself, who do you think will? So don't be afraid to toot your own horn when you've done something worth tooting about.

10. Every successful person has a very large ego. [Interviewer: "Every successful person? Mother Teresa? Jesus Christ?"] Far greater egos than you will ever understand.

11. It pays to trust your instincts.

12. Trust your own common sense first.

13. Faith in yourself can prove to be a very powerful force.

14. Go with your gut. Being an entrepreneur is not a group effort. You have to trust yourself. There are inexplicable signs that can guide you to, or away from, certain deals and certain people.

15. My whole life is about winning. I don't lose often. I almost never lose.

16. Part of being a winner is knowing when enough is enough.

17. Winners . . . may have wild dreams, but it's better than having no dreams.

18. Being stubborn is a big part of being a winner.

19. Winners see problems as just another way to prove themselves.

20. What separates the winners from the losers is how a person reacts to each new twist of fate.

21. Brainpower is the ultimate leverage.

22. Empowerment comes with enlightenment.

23. If you want the best, you'd better be the best.

24. To me it's very simple: if you're going to be thinking anyway, you might as well think big.

25. Think Big and Kick Ass.

26. Get in, get it done, get it done right, and get out.

27. Sometimes when you start thinking about all the problems you've got, it's a good idea to focus a little on some of the positives of the situation.

28. You just have to be the kind of guy to get people to do things.

29. The more you know, the more you realize how much you don't know.

30. There are always buyers for the best.

31. One of the greatest brand-builders of all times was Attila the Hun. His brand preceded him so powerfully that opposing armies often surrendered before fighting him. Although he was the leader of the Huns from 434 to 453 A.D., people still speak of Attila today. ... Branding is a way of life, not an event. We know that it is the brand that enables us to fulfill our life's purpose, so it is worth our energy and time. ... Crooks have brands. Just look at Bernie Madoff and Charles Ponzi. The Army, Navy, and Marines all have 'great brands.'

32. Dress for your culture. The way we dress says a lot about us – before we ever say a word.

33. Let your guard down, but only on purpose. Offer a calculated nugget of information or a provocative opinion to see what the reaction will be. It's a good way to assess the folks across the table.

34. Be optimistic, but always be prepared for the worst. I'm actually a very cautious person, which is different from being a pessimistic person. Call it positive thinking with a lot of reality checks.

35. Time is something that cannot be replaced.

36. Chances are that you will never wake up to an adversity-free day.

37. I've faced tremendous adversity. It's something just about everyone can relate to.

38. Sometimes by losing a battle you find a new way to win the war.

39. When I hear the word 'no' it becomes a challenge to me.

40. The bigger the problem, the bigger your chance for greatness.

41. I am listed in the Guinness Book of World Records for the biggest financial turnaround in history. I don't recommend anyone aims for the same goal.

42. I really had to think in out-of-the-box ways to keep from being buried alive.

43. Problems are often opportunities in disguise.

44. Focus on the solution, not the problem!

45. Envision yourself as victorious.

46. Focus on objective insights and solutions.

47. Failure is not permanent.

48. It's not just intelligence or luck that gets us places, it's tenacity in the face of adversity.

49. Problems are a part of life and a big part of business. The bigger your business, the bigger your life, the bigger your problems are likely to be.

50. Losers give up.

51. Never Give Up!

52. Life's not for the timid. Life's about never giving up.

53. The worst thing you can possibly do in a deal is seem desperate to make it. That makes the other guy smell blood, and then you're dead. The best thing you can do is deal from strength, and leverage is the biggest strength you can have. Leverage is having something the other guy wants. Or better yet, needs. Or best of all, simply can't do without.

54. Faith is a bit like wisdom. People can help you along the way with it, but above all you have to develop it yourself.

55. Stick to what you know.

56. Know what you want ... but keep it to yourself until a strategically necessary moment.

57. I protect myself by being flexible. I never get too attached to one deal or one approach. For starters, I keep a lot of balls in the air, because most deals fall out, no matter how promising they seem at first. In addition, once I've made a deal, I always come up with at least a half dozen approaches to making it work, because anything can happen, even to the best-laid plans.

58. Be ready to fight for your rights, and all will be well.

59. Bullies may act tough, but they're really closet cowards. The only people bullies push around are the ones they know they can beat.

60. Confront a strong, competent person, and he'll fight back harder than ever. Confront a bully, and in most cases, he'll fold like a deck of cards.

61. People are really vicious, and no place they'd be more vicious than in their relationships with the opposite sex.

62. Man is the most vicious of all animals, and life is a series of battles ending in victory or defeat. You just can't let people make a sucker out of you.

63. Be paranoid, because they are gonna try to fleece you.

64. Robert Moses ... said something that stayed with me ... 'You can't make an omelet without breaking eggs.' ... You can't build a skyscraper without breaking a few heads.

65. Believe me, you will have problems! It doesn't matter if your name is Trump or not, we all experience these things. Expect it!

66. Every day is a challenge, and every day is great.

67. Courage isn't the absence of fear, it's the conquering of fear.

68. Overcoming tremendous obstacles is all in a day's work – if you love what you're doing.

69. Work despite your fears, and very often they will disappear.

70. The higher you aim, the more opposition you will encounter. The more opposition you encounter ... the more energy you get.

71. If you want to be lucky, prepare for something big.

72. If you see big problems, look for big opportunities.

73. Get the right people to work with you.

74. Keeping yourself as diverse as possible can open you up to many more opportunities than you might imagine. Sometimes one thing can lead to another.

75. When your wardrobe malfunctions in front of 10,000 people, make it part of your act.

76. Ignorance is more expensive than education and using your brains.

77. Nothing is easy. Sometimes you just have to be stubborn.

78. Every challenge or obstacle you come up against is simply an opportunity in disguise.

79. Don't get complacent – thinking you're foolproof is a good way to set yourself up for a big mistake.

80. Try and replace negatives with positives, and you'll have more successes waiting for you, even if right now they're nowhere in sight.

81. The higher you aim, the more opposition you will encounter.

82. The more opposition you encounter ... the more energy you get!

83. Problem solving is much easier if you think of problems as challenges.

84. I don't believe the customer is always right.

85. Don't keep catering to complainers. A complainer will always be a complainer.

86. Don't believe the critics unless they love your work.

87. Not everything is going to work ... you may have to try a lot of things to get just one thing to work. That's tenacity.

88. Leaders are those who have replaced fear with discernment, which means they can predict the inevitable.

89. I have learned that what is essential can sometimes by invisible to the eye. That's where discernment comes.

90. Ask yourself: What am I pretending not to see?

91. It takes a lot of smarts to play dumb.

92. It's lonely at the top – but not crowded.

93. People who are capable of thinking for themselves will rarely be part of any herd.

94. The best way to have an edge is to live on one.

95. Passion is the number one ingredient [in resistance to change]. It can overcome many difficulties and so- called impossibilities. Getting anything started requires passion. Your enthusiasm can convince others to go along and see things your way. Resistance can be good if it gets you to improve your idea.

When someone can discourage you, you probably aren't determined enough. Be resolute. That's what it takes to get things done.

96. Without passion you don't have energy; without energy you have nothing.

97. Genuine enthusiasm is hard to beat.

98. To be done right, every job requires passion.

99. Passion gives you the intestinal fortitude you need to never give up.

100. Passion is more important than brains or talent.

101. You have to bring your ideas down to earth. Take your ideas and add the weight of passion to them as soon as possible before they disappear into thin air.

102. You have to love what you do. Without passion, great success is hard to come by. An entrepreneur will have tough times if he or she isn't passionate about what they're doing. People who love what they're doing don't give up. It's never even a consideration. It's a pretty simple formula.

103. I have seen some really talented, brainy people fail because of lack of passion.

104. If it seems too good to be true, it is.

105. Life is difficult no matter what, but hard work and perseverance make it a lot easier.

106. I'd rather be effective than just tidy.

107. Look for opportunities in every climate.

108. To be a major player in the world arena, pay attention and go the extra mile – every single day. Don't wait for opportunity to come to you.

109. Thoroughness is not a choice; it is a prerequisite.

110. Elevate your life to where it should be.

111. I don't accept excuses. Winners take control by accepting responsibility.

112. Creative people don't need to be motivated by anyone else. They motivate themselves.

113. Creativity and control can go hand in hand.

114. Thinking expansively is just another way to innovate.

115. My father used to tell us this story about a guy who loved soda, so he went into the soda business with a product he called 3UP. It failed. So he started again with a soda called 4UP. It failed, too. So, he decided to name his product 5UP and worked just as hard to make it work., but sure enough, it

failed again. He realized that he still loved soda, so he tried again with a product called 6UP. It failed, and he gave up completely. Then, few years later, someone else came up with a soda product and named it 7UP, which became a huge success.

116. If something is going to affect your life, it's best to know as much as you can about it.

117. If you look at the back of a beautiful and priceless tapestry, all you will see is a bunch of knots ... Sometimes that's all people will see because they haven't seen the finished design on the other side yet.

118. Developing your talents requires work, and work creates luck.

119. Precision, instinct and tempo are all necessary in order to become extraordinary.

120. Read as much as you can, learn as much as you can, every day.

121. Raise the bar on yourself. Never settle for doing 'enough.'

122. Don't sleep any more than you have to. I usually sleep about four hours per night.

123. I have friends who are successful and sleep ten hours a night, and I ask them, 'How can you compete against people like me if I sleep only four hours?' It rarely can be done. No matter how brilliant you are, there's not enough time in the day.

124. Don't make the mistake I did. Stay focused.

125. You can't get by on experience or smarts. Even the best surgeons need to be retrained regularly.

126. Before the dream lifts you into the clouds, make sure you've looked hard at the facts on the ground.

127. Bullsh*t will only get you so far.

128. A hundred years ago if someone replied, 'I want to walk on the moon' they might be considered a wacko.

129. Faith keeps you going with confidence and keeps you humble at the same time.

130. Studying history has made me very humble, because I know I'll never know it all.

131. Sometimes the picture is clearer if you're not in the picture at all.

132. Never underestimate the power of awareness.

133. No healthy person wants to be a burden to someone else.

134. We all have something to offer, every person is unique. ... I don't accept excuses.

135. The best negotiators are chameleons.

136. In a good negotiation, all sides win.

137. A good negotiator must be flexible to be successful.

138. No one can do it for you.

139. Pick up the phone and make sure they hear the sincerity in your voice. E-mail is for wimps.

140. It's often to your advantage to be underestimated.

141. It's often necessary to boast, but it's even better if others do.

142. The best way to impress people is through results.

143. Friends are good, but family is better.

144. Treat each decision like a lover.

145. I wasn't satisfied just to earn a good living. I was looking to make a statement.

146. The best is a quest.

147. You can create luck.

148. When you see a trend you don't like, change it!

149. A slow starter is always the fastest finisher.

150. Learning is a new beginning we can give ourselves every day.

151. A know-it-all is like a closed door.

152. Trust your own common sense first.

153. The worst thing you can do is be timid.

154. We can learn from our mistakes, but it's better to learn from our successes.

155. Most people want what's best for themselves, not for you. If those people have already spent a great deal of effort on their homework, why should they share it with you?

156. Good people equals good management and good management equals good people.

157. Never let someone's job title be the sole indication of their worth.

158. No matter how defeated you may feel, you've still got a chance. But it won't happen by itself. Get to work!

159. Power is not just about calling all the shots. It's about ability.

160. If you're careful about what you reveal, you'll have more flexibility.

161. I'm too busy to be devious.

162. A great Palm Beach lawyer called me a reverse tornado – I build everything in my path, instead of destroying it.

163. You have to bring your ideas down to earth. Take your ideas and add the weight of passion to them as soon as possible before they disappear into thin air.

164. I always go into a deal anticipating the worst. If you plan for the worst – if you can live with the worst – the good will always take care of itself.

165. You can't be imaginative or entrepreneurial if you've got too much structure.

166. I'm not too big on parties, because I can't stand small talk. Unfortunately, they're part of doing business.

167. There is nothing to compare with family if they happen to be competent, because you can trust family in a way you can never trust anyone else.

168. There are two things I've found I'm very good at: overcoming obstacles and motivating good people to do their best work.

169. Be optimistic, but always be prepared for the worst. I'm actually a very cautious person, which is different from being a pessimistic person. Call it positive thinking with a lot of reality checks.

170. Negative thinking stems from low self-esteem.

171. What's the point of having great knowledge and keeping it to yourself?

172. I like to think I have that instinct. That's why I don't hire a lot of number-crunchers, and I don't trust fancy marketing surveys. I do my own surveys and draw my own conclusions. I'm a great believer in asking everyone for an opinion before I make a decision. It's a natural reflex. If I'm thinking of buying a piece of property, I'll ask the people who live nearby about the area – what they think of the schools and the crime and the shops. When I'm in another city and I take a cab, I'll always make it a point to ask the cab-driver questions. I ask and I ask and I ask, until I begin to get a gut feeling about something. And that's when I make a decision.

173. One of the keys to thinking big is total focus. I think of it almost as a controlled neurosis, which is a quality I've noticed in many highly successful

entrepreneurs. They're obsessive, they're driven, they're single-minded and sometimes they're almost maniacal, but it's all channeled into their work. Where other people are paralyzed by neurosis, the people I'm talking about are actually helped by it.

[Money/Wealth]

1. You can have loads of money, but if you're not in good health, it's not so great.

2. Money has its limitations.

3. Wealth comes from within.

4. There is no advantage to being poor. In fact, poverty becomes a burden to everyone in the long run.

5. Education is a money machine.

6. When you have a lot of money, it can cause misery. But I'd rather have that kind of misery than the misery without it.

7. Let me tell you something. It's good to be thought of as poor right now [in the midst of his disastrous economic fallout period – "They think you're finished."]. You wouldn't believe some of the deals I'm making! I guess I have a perverse personality.

8. Being rich isn't a passive state.

9. Money is like talent. It doesn't do much good if you keep it to yourself.

10. In a world of more than six billion people, there are only 587 billionaires. It's an exclusive club. Would you like to join us?

11. Billionaires don't care what the odds are.

12. Part of thinking like a billionaire is thinking about those billions when you'll be gone.

13. We follow our vision, no matter how crazy or idiotic other people think it is.

14. Money is not an end in itself, but it's sometimes the most effective way to help us realize our dreams.

15. I don't do it for the money. I've got enough, much more than I'll ever need. I do it to do it. Deals are my art form.

16. Money, like comedy, is all about timing.

17. Due diligence equals increasing your financial IQ daily.

18. He who has the gold makes the rules.

19. Not teaching your kids about money is like not caring whether they eat.

20. One area you can never stop working on in life is your money.

21. We're all going to die. Money can't stop that.

[Elitism]

1. Elitism is a good thing, people.

2. I want you to become part of an elite wealth building team that works under my direction. Trust me, you are going to want to be part of this team. [In a pitch email for Trump University].

3. Why are they elite?" [the enclosed wealthy, cultural clique] "I have a much better apartment than they do. I'm smarter than they are. I'm richer than they are. I became president, and they didn't. And I'm representing the greatest, smartest, most loyal, best people on earth—the deplorables [the unfortunates, the wretched]."

4. My elite is better than the old elite.

5. The best thing about me is that I'm rich.

[Business]

1. In college, while my friends were reading the comics and the sports pages of newspapers, I was reading the listings of FHA foreclosures.

2. Real estate is like oxygen. It keeps me going when I'm awake, and it keeps me going when I'm asleep.

3. Even when I'm playing golf, I'm doing business. I never stop, and I'm usually having fun.

4. I'm America's most successful businessman. And I made a lot of money in the casino business. I've done things nobody thought could be done. And I've got big plans.

5. Everything I do in life is framed through the view of a businessman. That's my instinct.

6. Vision is my best asset; I know what sells and I know what people want.

7. No matter how good you are, timing is so important; and some people have timing, and some people don't, and I have it.

8. Some people aren't meant to be rich. ... It's just something you have, something you're born with. Most people don't have the ability to be rich, because they're too lazy or they don't have the desire or the stick-to-itiveness. It's a talent. Some people have a talent for piano. Some people have a talent for raising a family. Some people have a talent for golf. I just have a talent for making money.

9. My own style of conducting business is straightforward. I think big. I aim very high, and then I keep pushing and pushing towards that goal – and beyond it.

10. I'm not big on compromise. I understand compromise. Sometimes compromise is the right answer, but oftentimes compromise is the equivalent of defeat, and I don't like being defeated.

11. I almost lost everything in the early 90s, but I got through it all and survived and thrived.

12. When I got no answer and a few more months had gone by, I wrote again and said I'd love to drop by and see him again. More time passed, and I wrote another letter, suggesting a whole new way to make the deal. I was relentless, even in the face of a total lack of encouragement, because much more often than you'd think, sheer persistence is the difference between success and failure.

13. It's usually fun being The Donald, but in the early 1990s I was many billions in the red, 975 million of that debt I personally guaranteed. The banks for were crawling all over me. Then the Gulf War had a disastrous effect on tourism. Cash flows were dwindling at my casinos. Then I missed a mortgage payment on the Castle in Atlantic City. All hell broke loose. Wall Street went nuts. The newspapers screamed at my demise. I was up against the wall. So I sold a few assets to stay afloat. Then, after being pummeled by my bankers, Ivana turned around and sued me for $2 billion. Life, I thought, looked bleak. ... As bad as things got for me – and they got pretty bad – I never let anyone push me around.

Then, one day around Christmas of 1990 I said to myself, Donald, it's time to fight back. So, I got down to work. Today I'm over $3 billion in the black. I've paid off my personal debt, business is great, I'm single (and available!), and I'm loving life.

As a result of these experiences, my thinking has changed. I'm sharper. I believe in an eye for an eye – like the Old Testament says. Some of the people who forget to lift a finger when I needed them, when I was down, they need my help now and I'm screwing them against the wall. I'm doing a number ... and I'm having so much fun. People say that's not nice, but I really believe in getting even.

On the other hand, there were those I wouldn't have completely counted on who were loyal to the nth degree. These people were not only loyal, they were warriors. They supported me and saw me through – These are the people I learned to rely on.

14. You know where the real jungle lives? Manhattan, New York city. That's my jungle and that's the real jungle. There're more snakes here and more things that can kill you here.

15. This island is the real jungle. If you're not careful, it can chew you up and spit you out. But if you work hard, you can really hit it big, and I mean really big.

16. New York. My city. Where the wheels of the global economy never stop turning. A concrete metropolis of unparalleled strength and purpose that drives the business world. Manhattan is a tough place. York. My city. Where the wheels of the global economy never stop turning. A concrete metropolis of unparalleled strength and purpose that drives the business world. Manhattan is a tough place. This island is the real jungle. If you're not careful, it can chew you up and spit you out. But if you work hard, you can really hit it big, and I mean really big.

17. Sometimes, part of making a deal is denigrating your competition.

18. ["It was the part of the deal Donald loved, that touch of moral Larceny."] This is one of the best deals I ever made in my life. I really, really whipped this guy, really took this sucker for some big money.

19. I want the assholes out of here. I want the incompetence out of here. I want people in here who are going to kick some ass. I want pricks. What I need are more nasty pricks in this company. Warriors.

20. I've built an incredible company. I went to a great school. I came out – I built an incredible company. I wrote the number one selling business book of all time: *Trump: The Art of the Deal*.

21. If you have to lie, cheat, and steal, you're just not doing it right. ... My career is a model of tough, fair dealing and fantastic success – without shortcuts, without breaking the law.

22. Maybe tackiness is at the heart of corporate corruption. ... But, as I prove every day, it doesn't have to be that way at all.

23. I'm not a diplomat who wants everybody else to be happy. I'm a practical businessman who has learned that when you believe in something, you never stop, you never quit, and if you get knocked down, you climb right back and keep fighting until you win. That's been my strategy all my life and I've been very successful following it.

24. I would probably choose love over work. [were he forced to choose one or the other]. ... When I say love, I'm also saying it in the positive sense that I also consider my work to be love.

25. I truly believe that someone successful is never really happy, because dissatisfaction is what drives him. I've never met a successful person who wasn't neurotic. It's not a terrible thing; it's controlled neuroses.

26. Controlled neuroses means having a tremendous energy level, an abundance of discontent that often isn't visible. It's also not oversleeping. I don't sleep more than four hours a night. I have friends who need twelve hours a night and I tell them they're at a major disadvantage in terms of playing the game.

27. [Interviewer: "Don't you think, if I give you a million dollars, you owe me something for that."] You know what? That's true, but, I'll tell you, it gets a lot tougher when you have to announce, perhaps, on the Internet or in various forms of whatever announcement that so-and-so gave a lot of money to such-and-such a candidate; then, it's a lot tougher.

I mean, I had Ed Koch tell me that I can't – that he can't do something for me because I was a contributor to his campaign. And I never liked him after that, to be honest with you.

I said: "You mean, I would have been better off being an enemy." He said: 'Well, I don't know how you ... ' I said: "You mean, I contribute to your campaign, and now you can't help me with something because I was a contributor. I'm much better off not contributing. So, there is that."

28. You don't have to be beautiful to work for me – just be good at your job. I've been accused of admiring beautiful women. I plead guilty. But when it comes to the workplace, anyone who is beautiful had better have brains, too. You need competent people with an inherent work ethic. I'm not a complacent person and I can't have a complacent staff. I move forward quickly and so must they.

29. I called myself the king of debt. I'm the king of debt. I'm great with debt, nobody knows debt better than me. I made a fortune by using debt. And if things don't work out I renegotiate the debt, I mean that's a smart thing not a stupid thing. And I made a fortune.

30. I fight like hell to pay [taxes] as little for two reasons. Number one, I'm a businessman. And that's the way you're supposed to do it. ... The other reason is that I hate the way our government spends our taxes. I hate the way they waste our money. Trillions and trillions of dollars of waste and abuse. And I hate it.

31. Most of us need letters of recommendation now and then. I write them as well as receive them, and I always look for the words "responsible, professional, and loyal." If you can build your reputation on three words, those would be three at the top to choose from. I also think of those words when it

comes to the Trump brand – to be authentic when it comes to responsibility, professionalism, and loyalty – to my buyers, clients, students, readers, audiences, and so forth. I'll be the first to admit it's not always easy. I am responsible for a lot of people. But high standards are high standards, and that's what I stand for. I will not accept less from myself.

32. [Interviewer: How far are you willing to push adversaries?"] I will demand anything I can get. When you're doing business, you take people to the brink of breaking them without having them break, to the maximum point their heads can handle – without breaking them. That's the sign of a good businessman: Somebody else would take them fifteen steps beyond their breaking point.

33. A great golf course gives you great power.

[Politics]

1. Everything I do in life is framed through the view of a businessman. That's my instinct.

2. I can't wait to see what I'll become involved in next!

3. People have always asked me if I ever be involved in politics. Seems every so often there is some unfounded rumor that I'm considering seeking office – even the presidency! The problem is, I think I'm too honest, and perhaps too controversial, to be a politician. I always say it like it is, and I'm not sure that a politician can do that, although I might just be able to get away with it because people tend to like me. And therefore, despite all the polls that say I should run I would probably not be a very successful politician.

4. I would center my presidency on three principles: one term, two-fisted policies, and no excuses. For voters it would be a business approach, and the best one available in the presidential marketplace. I'd lead by example. And what I could also bring to the presidency is a new spirit, a great spirit that we haven't had in this country for a long time – the kind of spirit that built the American Dream.

5. I would never lie [referring to the American people]. ... I would not lie. I absolutely would not lie.

6. What do you have to lose by trying something new like Trump? What do you have to lose? You're living in poverty; your schools are no good; you have no jobs; 58 percent of your youth is unemployed. What the hell do you have to lose?

7. [Tried to reach out to Latino voters on Cinco de Mayo by tweeting a picture of a taco bowl, saying:] "I love Hispanics. ... The best taco bowls are made in Trump Tower Grill. I love Hispanics!"

8. I have made the tough decisions, always with an eye toward the bottom line. Perhaps it's time America was run like a business.

9. We need someone with a proven track record in business who understands greatness, someone who can rally us to standard of excellence we once epitomized and explain what needs to be done.

10. I am shaking up the establishment on both sides of the political aisle.

11. Our country doesn't win anymore.

12. I have a nasty habit that most career politicians don't have, because I can't be bought. I tell the truth. I'm not afraid to say exactly what I believe. When I'm asked a question, I don't answer with a speech that ignores a controversial subject. I answer the question. Sometimes people don't like my answers. Too bad. So they attack me.

13. I think the only difference between me and the other candidates is that I'm more honest and my women are more beautiful.

14. That's true. [regarding breaking the rules of how candidates usually act.] That, I agree with you. They say there's never been anything like this.

15. I'm not playing by the usual status-quo rules.

16. No one is paying me to say these things. I am paying my own way, And I'm not beholden to any special interests and lobbyists.

17. My life is seeing everything in terms of "How would *I* handle that? Look at the war in Iraq and the mess that we're in. I would never have handled it that way. Does anybody really believe that Iraq is going to be a wonderful democracy where people are going to run down to the voting box and gently put in their ballot and the winner is happily going to step up to lead the county? C'mon. Two minutes after we leave, there's going to be a revolution, and the meanest, toughest, smartest, most vicious guy will take over. And he'll have weapons of mass destruction, which Saddam didn't have.

18. One of the key problems today is that politics is such a disgrace, good people don't go into government.

19. A lot of times when I speak, people say I don't provide specific policies that some pollster has determined are what people want to hear. I know that's not the way professional politicians do it – they seem to poll and focus-group every word.

20. I ask people to look at what I've done throughout my whole career. Look at how successful I've been doing things my way. So, they have a choice. They can pretend some impossible solution is actually going to happen, or they can listen to the person who has proved that he can solve problems.

21. I never worry about being politically correct. I don't need to read the polls to make my decisions. And I don't see any reason to change my approach.

22. The special interests and lobbyists ... I do not take a penny from those people. I'm paying my own way. So the old rules don't apply to me – and those people who benefit from those rules don't know how to react. At first, they hoped if they ignored me I would go away.

23. Maybe the journalists' most embarrassing moment so far came when I filed my financial statement. I am the richest presidential candidate in history. I'm the only billionaire ever to run. I'm not accepting donations from my rich friends, special interests, or lobbyists. When was the last time someone running for political office didn't take Money? The voters know it – and love it.

24. That has always been my philosophy: If my critics attack me, then I'll fight back. Let's be honest and truthful with one another. I'm confident my answer makes the most sense.

25. You know who really appreciates this approach? The American people.

26. They're not used to hearing the truth from politicians, but they love it, and they love hearing it from me.

27. I don't know who Putin is.

28. Look at Putin – What's he doing with Russia? – I mean, you know, what's going on over there. I mean this guy has done – whether like him or don't like him – He's doing a great job.

29. I have no relationship with [Putin] other than he called me a genius.

30. Putin likes me.

31. I have nothing to do with Russia whatsoever.

32. I would love to be able to get along with Russia and I think they'd like to be able to get along with us. It's in our mutual interest. And I don't go in with any preconceived notion, but I will tell you, I would say – when they used to say, during the campaign, Donald Trump loves Putin, Putin loves Donald Trump, I said, huh, wouldn't it be nice, I'd say this in front of thousands of people, wouldn't it be nice to actually report what they said, wouldn't it be nice if we actually got along with Russia, wouldn't it be nice if we went after ISIS together, which is, by the way, aside from being dangerous, it's very expensive, and ISIS shouldn't have been even allowed to form, and the people will stand up and give me a massive hand. You know they thought it was bad that I was getting along with Putin or that I believe strongly if we can get along with Russia that's a positive thing. It is a great thing that we can get along with not only Russia but that we get along with other countries.

33. Look, we have people that are chopping off heads and drowning people in steel cages and we're not allowed to waterboard.

34. They have never seen anyone like me in politics. They have never seen anyone who is willing to stand up to the lobbyists, the PACs, the special interests, who all have way too much influence over Washington politicians. I am paying my own way so I can say what I want. I will only do what is right for our country, which I love.

35. The basic difference between the politician's way and my way is that I've actually had to do the things that politicians only talk about doing.

36. Why do you think people tune in [when I'm on TV]? The fact is I give people what they need and deserve to hear – exactly what they don't get from politicians – and that is The Truth. Our country is a mess right now and we don't have time to pretend otherwise. We don't have time to waste on being politically correct.

37. You listen to the politicians and it's as if they are speaking from a script titled "How Boring Can I Possibly Be?" They're so afraid of tripping on their own words, terrified that they're going to say something unscripted and go off message – that's the phrase they use, "go off message" – that they are verbally paralyzed. They'll do anything they can to avoid answering a question--and the media plays the game with them.

38. If there's one thing I've learned from dealing with politicians over the years, it's that the only thing guaranteed to force them into action is the press – or, more specifically, fear of the press.

39. I dealt with Gaddafi [former Libya ruler]. I rented him a piece of land. He paid me more for one night than the land was worth for two years, and then I didn't let him use the land. That's what we should be doing. I don't want to use the word "screwed," but I screwed him. That's what we [United States government] should be doing.

40. For evangelicals, for the Christians, for the everybody, for everybody of religion, this will be, may be, the most important election that our country has ever had. And once I get in, I will do my thing that I do very well. And I figure it is probably, maybe the only way I'm going to get to heaven. So, I better do a good job.

41. I will be the greatest job President that God ever created.

42. I don't necessarily say things that are so correct. If you look at *The Apprentice* [his popular TV reality show], as an example, 'I'm not very politically correct.'"

43. I'm just thinking to myself right now, we should just cancel the election [for the Presidency] and just give it to Trump, right?

[Religion]

1. God is in my life every day.

2. In business I don't actively make decisions based on my religious beliefs, but those beliefs are there – big time.

3. Nobody has done more for Christianity or for evangelicals or for religion itself than I have.

4. We go in church and when I drink my little wine, which is about the only wine I drink, and have my little cracker, I guess that is a form of asking for forgiveness. And I do that as often as possible, because I feel cleansed, OK? But, you know, to me, that is important, I do that."

5. There's no way I would ever ... do anything negative to a Bible. ... I would have a fear of doing something other than very positive.'"

6. I go [to church] as much as I can. Always on Christmas. Always on Easter. Always when there's a major occasion ... and during Sundays. I'm a Sunday church person. I'll go when I can.

7. I think my philosophy basically is there has to be something to this. I mean we just can't be put here for the sake of living our 60, 70, 80, 90, 100 years, whatever it might be, and just end up with nothing at the end of that time after all the combat, and I really look at life to a certain extent as combat. There has to be something. I mean we have to be in a test period or there has to be something after this. Otherwise, it just seems so futile.

8. Look deeply within yourself to discover your higher self – the essential you. Find out what you really want, what you truly value, and how far you'll go to get it. In this process, you'll also find out what you're made of. ... When we understand our higher selves it can help us become more visionary. Unfortunately, the word visionary may evoke a negative image such as being a castle builder or a Don Quixote – someone with unrealistic dreams. However, it's fine to be a dreamer provided you're also realistic. Visionaries move the world and create new dimensions. Look at Bill Gates in technology and Mark Burnett in reality television, or Pablo Picasso, Igor Stravinsky, and other great artists. Each followed his vision and enriched the world.

9. [On being metaphysical] No.

10. Life is very fragile. Anything can change, without warning, and that's why I try not to take any of what's happened too seriously.

11. There has to be a reason we are here. What are we doing? You know there is an expression: "Life is what you do while you're waiting to die." ... There has to be a reason that we're going through this. There has to be a reason for everything. I do believe in God. I think they're just has to be something that's far greater than us.

12. I believe we come on earth maybe as a testing period, and maybe for whatever reason. I guess again that goes back to the mind with a 1 percent and the 3 percent, that we could expand the 3 percent of the use of the mind maybe we'd be able to figure out what happens afterwards, but we probably will not be able to figure that out.

13. I think my philosophy basically is there has to be something to this. I mean we just can't be put here for the sake of living our 60, 70, 80, 90, 100 years, whatever it might be, and just end up with nothing at the end of that time after all the combat, and I really look at life to a certain extent as combat. There has to be something. I mean we have to be in a test period or there has to be something after this. Otherwise, it just seems so futile.

14. Look deeply within yourself to discover your higher self – the essential you. Find out what you really want, what you truly value, and how far you'll go to get it. In this process, you'll also find out what you're made of. ... When we understand our higher selves it can help us become more visionary. Unfortunately, the word visionary may evoke a negative image such as being a castle builder or a Don Quixote – someone with unrealistic dreams. However, it's fine to be a dreamer provided you're also realistic. Visionaries move the world and create new dimensions. Look at Bill Gates in technology and Mark Burnett in reality television, or Pablo Picasso, Igor Stravinsky, and other great artists. Each followed his vision and enriched the world.

15. We're here and we live our sixty, seventy or eighty years and we're gone. You win, you win, and in the end, it doesn't mean a hell of a lot. But it is something to do-to keep you interested.

16. Who knows what's in the deepest part of my mind.

17. Join the Explorer's Club. Learn about the mysteries of life.

[Contradictions]

INTRODUCTORY NOTES CONCERNING SUBTLETIES OF CONTRADICTIONS

I include these introductory notes because of the intellectual, psychological, and rhetorical complexities underlying contradictions when employed for purpose of persuasion.

COMMENTS BY RELIABLE SOURCES REGARDING TRUMP'S CONTRADICTIONS

1. "Consistency, Emerson said, is the hobgoblin of little minds. Perhaps no one in American public life channels this thought more than Donald J. Trump. He not only doesn't fear contradiction, he embraces it. And he is downright scornful of those little minds that are bothered by his performances."

2. "Donald Trump likes to say that he 'tells it like it is,' and his blunt style has won him the Republican nomination, buoyed by voters who like feeling they know just where a candidate stands on the issues. So where *does* he stand? Over the past four decades Trump has talked about every imaginable subject: gun rights to germs, the nature of competition to pre-nuptial agreements, love and sex, self-promotion and politics. And on every one of those topics, he has taken positions that directly contradict *exactly what he has previously said.*"

3. "In a world where candidates have lost elections over a single flip-flop, Trump has turned the self-contradiction into an art form. To create the definitive archive of Trump's long argument with himself, *Politico* mined an almost limitless seam of his radio and TV interviews, newspaper and magazine profiles, books written about him and books written by him, rambling campaign speeches and late-night tweets. Read them together and they reveal a person who may be amazingly good at gauging the moment, but whose principles, beyond simply winning, remain elusive – perhaps even to himself."

4. "Mr. Trump's willingness to be inconsistent – even in a single interview, or the same speech – has baffled political strategists for months. Even more puzzling is his followers' happy toleration of it. It is as though the content of what Mr. Trump says doesn't matter; only the fact that he is saying it does. But how could that be? After all, other candidates are seemingly held to different standards, by their supporters and others. They are held responsible for what they say.

"A striking early example of this was Mr. Trump's initial refusal to condemn the Ku Klux Klan and other white nationalists who had been endorsing him. Mr. Trump later denounced such groups. Yet many white supremacists, including David Duke, continue to support Mr. Trump. Why?

"The explanation, I think, lies in the power of contradictions themselves. That power, and Mr. Trump's effective use of it, tells us as much about ourselves and our culture's attitude toward truth as it tells us about him.

"From the standpoint of classical logic and mathematics, what's bad about a contradiction is that it leads to absurdity. You can derive any proposition you wish from a contradiction in a few simple steps. Yet that's precisely what makes them so useful from the point of view of political psychology – indeed, the more blatant the contradiction the better.

"Of course, politicians often "walk back" comments – either because they misspoke, or because [they] interpret evidence so that it conforms to what we already believe. Walking a comment back says you are taking responsibility for what you've said. Blatant contradiction puts the responsibility back onto the shoulders of the listener. If I simply deny what I earlier affirmed and act as if nothing has happened, then *you* are left having to decide what I really meant. And psychology, as well as common sense, tells us that human beings are prone to "confirmation bias." That is, we tend to interpret evidence so that it conforms to what we already believe.

"So if we like the Klan, we can read into Mr. Trump's remarks that he does, too. As so many of his followers put it, Mr. Trump is not afraid to "tell it like it is." Yet when faced with a contradiction, the "it" can be up to you.

"So while he sometimes does massage his own statements – as he tried to do last month after his remarks on punishing women for getting abortions — Mr. Trump is most effective when he simply says the opposite of what he said before. In part, that's because Mr. Trump's contradictions are loud and confident. ("I love Hispanics!" he tweeted on Thursday, Cinco de Mayo, along with a picture of him with a taco bowl.) But it is also because when a person says something as well as its opposite, his listeners can infer that he *really believes* whichever statement they wish him to believe.

"That contradictions are particularly useful to Mr. Trump also tells us something about what some people find appealing about him. Indeed, it reveals an even deeper contradiction. Mr. Trump's explicit lack of authenticity is what makes him so authentic. He is like a walking oxymoron (which is perhaps not surprising, given that reality TV is the medium in which he has most flourished). To some, that he is contradicting himself so freely shows that he really doesn't care what "they" (read: the news media, liberals, women, minorities) think. The signal this sends is one of strength: Only the strong can afford not to care.

"There is also a deeper philosophical issue here. The most disturbing power of contradiction is that its repeated use can dull our sensitivity to the value of truth itself. That's particularly so given that most Americans live in a digital world that both makes it easier and harder to figure out what is true. Googling is like being in a room with a million shouting voices. It is only natural that we'll hear those voices that are most similar to our own, shouting what we already believe, and as a result Google can find you confirmation for almost anything, no matter how absurd.

"Of course, we are aware that those with different views can do the same. And that very fact, if we aren't careful, can lead us into thinking that objectivity is a "dead value." We get so used to contradictory information, rival sources, that we find ourselves no longer valuing truth.

"In George Orwell's "1984," the protagonist is tortured until he agrees that two plus two equals five. The point, his torturer makes clear, is to make him see that there is no objective truth other than what the party says is true. That's the deep power of contradiction. Repeated enough, political contradictions can lull us into giving up on critical thought altogether. And once that happens, we risk giving up on truth. At which point contradictions – and everything other than power – will no longer matter."

Trump's Contradictions

[1]

I don't want to be provocative, and in many cases I try not to be provocative.
I do love provoking people. There is truth to that.

[2]
I avoid people with especially high opinions of their own abilities or worth.
I don't have to brag. I don't have to. Believe it or not
Hey, look, I went to the hardest school to get into, the best school in the world, I guess you could say, the Wharton School of Finance. It's like super genius stuff. I came out. I built a tremendous company. I had tremendous success.

[3]
Don't worry about actively promoting yourself.
Let people know what you've done. What good is it if no one knows about it? You've gotta be a promoter.
Everyone says, 'Oh, Trump is a great promoter.' I don't think I'm even a *good* promoter.

[4]
Subtlety and modesty are appropriate for nuns and therapists. So don't be afraid to toot your own horn when you've done something worth tooting about.
Publicity gradually dehumanizes you.

[5]
Everybody kisses your ass when you're hot. If you're not hot, they don't even call. So, it's always good to stay hot.

I hate people that think they're hot stuff, and they're nothing.

[6]
Anyone who thinks he's going to win them all is going to wind up a big loser.

I win, I win, I always win. In the end I always win, whether it's in golf, whether it's in tennis, whether it's in life, I just always win. And I tell people I always win, because I do.

[7]
I do whine, because I want to win, and I'm not happy about not winning, and I am a whiner, and I keep whining and whining until I win.

Sometimes you have to give up the fight and walk away, and move on to something that's more productive.

[8]
Remember that in the best negotiations, everyone wins.

You hear lots of people say that a great deal is when both sides win. That is a bunch of crap.

[9]
I learned from my father that work can make you happy.

I think of it almost as a controlled neurosis, which is a quality I've noticed in many highly successful entrepreneurs. They're obsessive, they're driven, they're single-minded and sometimes they're almost maniacal, but it's all channeled into their work. … I don't say this trait leads to a happier life, or a better life, but it's great when it comes to getting what you want.

[10]
Qadhafi in Libya is killing thousands of people, nobody knows how bad it is, and we're sitting around, we have soldiers, all over the Middle East, and we're not bringing 'em in to stop this horrible carnage. … We should go in, we should stop this guy, which would be very easy and very quick.

I never discussed that subject. I was in favor of Libya? We would be so much better off if Qadhafi were in charge right now.

[11]
Angela Merkel [chancellor of Germany] is doing a fantastic job. … Youth unemployment is at a record low & she has a budget surplus.

She's ruining Germany.

[12]
I would tax people of wealth, of great wealth, people over $10 million, by 14.25 percent.

[Asked about his tax cuts for billionaires on CNBC:] I am not necessarily a huge fan of that.

[13]
Compromise is not a dirty word.

I'm not big on compromise. I understand compromise. Sometimes compromise is the right answer, but oftentimes compromise is the equivalent of defeat, and I don't like being defeated.

[14]
I'm walking, talking proof of the American Dream. For me, the American Dream is not just a dream; it's a reality.

The American Dream is dead.

[15]
We are the greatest country the world has ever known.

Maybe we Americans pump ourselves up too much.

[16]
I read a lot ... and over my life, I've read so much.

I don't read much.

[17]
I see no value whatsoever in believing ignorance to be an attribute.

I love the poorly educated.

[18]
I've cultivated the learning habit over the years, and it's one of the most pleasurable aspects of my life.

All I know is what's on the Internet.

[19]
Fortunately, I don't pride myself on being a know-it-all.

It would take an hour and a half to learn everything there is to learn about missiles. ... I think I know most of it anyway.

[20]
I'm a thinker, and I have been a thinker. ... I'm a very deep thinker.

The day I realized it can be smart to be shallow was, for me, a deep experience.

[21]
Small talk can be one of the best ways to educate yourself.

I can't stand small talk.

[22]
Be tough, be smart, be personable, but don't take things personally.
When someone attacks me, I attack back. Hard.

[23]
But there is nothing better than having a great marriage, in my opinion. There is nothing more beautiful, and there is nothing more important.

You marry for love, but your signature on the marriage certificate is all about rights, duties, and property. It's a legally binding contract that knows nothing of love.

[24]
I think there are two Donald Trumps.
I don't think there are two Donald Trumps. I think there's one Donald Trump.

[25]
Sometimes – not often, but sometimes – less is more.
I always say, "More is more."

[26]
New York is a great place. It's got great people. It's got loving people, wonderful people.

You know where the real jungle lives? Manhattan, New York city. That's my jungle and that's the real jungle. There're more snakes here and more things that can kill you here.

[27]
Nobody owns me.
I'm owned by the people!

[28]
Eminent domain is wonderful.
I don't like eminent domain.

[29]
I do not condone violence in any shape.
If you see somebody getting ready to throw a tomato, knock the crap out of 'em, would you? Seriously. OK? Just knock the hell – I promise you, I will pay the legal fees, I promise, I promise.

[30]
I'm an environmentalist.
Global warming is a total, and very expensive, hoax!

[31]
I generally oppose gun control, but I support the ban on assault weapons and I support a slightly longer waiting period to purchase a gun.

I am the strongest person running in favor of the Second Amendment.

[32]
Women who get abortions should be punished.

Only doctors should be punished; women are victims.

If Congress were to pass legislation making abortion illegal and the federal courts upheld this legislation, or any state were permitted to ban abortion under state and federal law, the doctor or any other person performing this illegal act upon a woman would be held legally responsible, not the woman.

[33]
Millions and millions of women—cervical cancer, breast cancer—are helped by Planned Parenthood. So, you can say whatever you want, but they have millions of women going through Planned Parenthood that are helped greatly.

But Planned Parenthood should absolutely be defunded. I mean, if you look at what's going on with that, it's terrible.

[34]
I love the media. They're wonderful.

They are the most dishonest people in the world. The media. They are the worst. They are very dishonest people. They are terrible.

[35]
If you equivocate, it's an indication that you're unsure of yourself and what you're doing. It's also what politicians do all the time, and I find it inappropriate, insulting and condescending. I try not to do it.

I'm very capable of changing to anything I want to change to.

[36]
I believe in positive thinking, but I also believe in the power of negative thinking

I never think of the negative.

I always go into the deal anticipating the worst.

I don't think positively, I don't think negatively.

[37]
I'm one of those people who don't require a lot of sleep – maybe three or four hours a night. So, what do I do with those extra hours? I read.

I'm a guy who lies awake at night and thinks and plots.

[38]
I don't worry about anything.

Too many countries have nuclear weapons; nobody knows where they're all pointed, what button it takes to launch them. The bomb Harry Truman dropped on Hiroshima was a toy next to today's. We have thousands of weapons pointed at us and nobody even knows if they're going to go in the right direction. They've never really been tested. These jerks in charge don't know how to paint a wall, and we're relying on them to shoot nuclear missiles to Moscow. What happens if they don't go there? What happens if our computer systems aren't working? Nobody knows if this equipment works, and I've seen numerous reports lately stating that the probability is they don't work. It's a total mess.

[39]
I've never said I'm a perfect person, nor pretended to be someone that I'm not.
I consider myself too perfect and have no faults.

[40]
I'm a very untrusting guy.
I think maybe my greatest weakness is that I trust people too much. I'm too trusting.

[41]
[on being "a very shallow person"] That's one of my strengths. I never pretend to be anything else.
I am somebody with a lot of heart.

[42]
I cherish women. I want to help women. I'm going to be able to do things for women that no other candidate would be able to do.
Women, you have to treat them like s- - t.

[43]
(i) I don't have a racist bone in my body.

I've got to tell you something else. I think that the guy is lazy. Probably not his fault because this is a trait in Blacks. It really is, I believe that. ... Don't you agree? ... [in response to the remark that that kind of remark could be damaging to his image:] Yeah, you're right, if anybody ever heard me say that ... Holy s_ _t ... I'd be in a lot of trouble. But I have to tell you, that's the way I feel. ... It's a trait.

(ii) I am the least racist person there is. And I think most people that know me would tell you that. I am the least racist.

Black guys counting my money! I hate it. The only kind of people I want counting my money are little short guys that wear yarmulkes every day.

PART TWO

Revealed by Others and this Author

Character and Tactics Descriptions

*The quotations I present in **Part Two** by third persons support and question the veracity of Trump's self-proclaimed idol-supremacy both professionally and personally. They spotlight Trump's character and tactics from favorable to unfavorable to malicious aspects.*

1
FAVORABLE PERSPECTIVES

1. "He's a regular guy who speaks his mind, who goes against the establishment of time. He's sued New York how many times and won. This is a brilliant businessman that stands for what is great about our country, what makes America the best country in the world. He loves business and loves to orate about business he always tells me: 'You know where the real jungle lives? Manhattan, New York city. That's my jungle and that's the real jungle.'"

2. [Tony Senecal, former Trump butler] "First of all, he's an incredibly generous person. He's generous to his employees [and] he's generous to strangers. Most of the time he's just a nice man. I mean, I lasted with him for 20 years. He had to be pretty good."

3. "He's also very shrewd. Part of that shrewdness is an uncanny ability to make people believe that what he says is true, even as he engages in what he loves to call 'truthful hyperbole.' Even his closest friends know that he exaggerates, but they forgive him for it because they know he's not far off the mark, and he can be awfully persuasive."

4. "Usually braggarts come off as offensive, heavy-handed, and unpleasant to be around. 'With Donald, you never feel he's offensive. Even if he's bragging about himself, his properties, it's light, comical, never taken very seriously. One of his big advantages is that people like him a lot. If people like you, that's half the business."

5. "He's brazen. He fears nothing."

6. "To be a celebrity is very unique. I know a lot of people with money but they can never transform themselves into celebrities. ... It takes a look. ... The certain personality – not always necessarily even a good personality, but a unique personality."

7. "When Donald Trump says, 'I'm worth $5 billion,' the New York sophisticate doesn't take it seriously."

8. "As sneering as this journalist is toward Donald Trump [his cynical review of Trump's authenticity and character], such venom has had no effect on the man. If all journalists thought like this cynical one, Trump would have been a mere footnote in business history, not the resilient, creative titan he has turned out to be. Indeed, in journalism, claiming to have their eyes just as wide open as the cynical journalist's, are forgiving of Trump's flaws – perhaps because they feel that so much of what he says is close to the truth, if not the truth itself."

9. "But a more compelling explanation for the gentility displayed toward his flights into exaggeration is his reputation as an honest businessman." 'He might be accused of using too much creative hyperbole, too much press pageantry, but I've never heard him accused privately or openly of being dishonest – never once.'"

10. "First of all he's extremely successful – Even when he's down and out. He's got a charm and charisma and he's very good to friends. This is a man who tells you what he thinks, and I think people respond very strongly to that. He's one of a kind, and we don't have very many of them."

11. "The thing I don't get is why his buildings fetch premiums. I can't explain it. Some have nice views. But why is he so popular? People are fascinated by him. He's not just making it up. I'd like to think he's creating it. But go down to the communities; they love him."

12. "He's not purporting to be anything beyond what he is. He is what he is. He's a high-class, Wharton-educated, brilliant con man. And I think he's the best at it."

13. "It's the force of his personality that makes him such a great salesman."

14. "One reason people take to Trump is his ability to get them on his side."

15. "He is great at flattery. Even he knows that he can talk about himself for only so long without turning people off. So, he tries to make a visitor to his office or a caller on the phone feel very important. That makes it harder not to warm up to trump and become loyal to the Trump brand."

16. "We [Trump's sister and father] don't dazzle. Donald dazzles. He really has the whole package."

17. "You are a unique personality that is capable of doing the impossible." [Egyptian President Abdel Fattah el Sisi, in Saudia Arabia for a summit on fighting terrorism, told the U.S. leader]

18. "[He's] magnetic. He has an ability to capture people. He's got such a commanding presence."

19. "It is indeed a commanding presence, at the size of some professional basketball guards, 6 feet, 3 inches tall; a solid build, that shock of blond hair; and a slow almost methodical gait. He requires most people – those under his height – to look up at him. That automatically gives him an advantage. Then there is the brusqueness of his speech. He speaks passionately about almost everything. Almost every comment."

20. "He's got the women and the money; and, by the way, he also has great children. He very often says what he thinks, even [if] and what he says isn't politically correct, and will get him in trouble."

21. "Trump certainly appeared to have many of the traits of a politician. People recognized him on the street. Most of those who met him seemed to like him. Some worshipped him. He had charisma. He was a household name. He thought his popularity and celebrity stemmed from being antipolitical, 'Maybe more because I don't necessarily say things that are so correct. If you look at *The Apprentice* [his popular TV reality show], as an example, 'I'm not very politically correct.'"

22. "Through his intense and aggressive efforts, he has elevated self-promotion to a critical business strategy, and no one does it better."

23. "Trump is not an entertainer. He is a charismatic businessman. He's a great communicator. If Donald wasn't that showy and flamboyant, I wouldn't have asked him to be my partner. You can't have someone worth a few billion dollars be a wallflower and have nothing to say. It wouldn't work with this kind of program ["The Apprentice"]. You need a billionaire who is charismatic and communicates very well."

24. "To understand how Donald Trump functions in business, one should think of him not necessarily as an entertainer, but rather as someone with the skills of an entertainer … especially as an actor – and he gets very far with those skills."

25. "Instead of relying on public-relations specialists either inside or outside his organization, he, in effect, has become his own public-relation agency. These specialists from time to time advise him to steer clear of the media, and he did not want to heed such advice. More than any other business leader of his era, he understood the business necessity of whipping up a public-relations storm around his name and his projects."

"By thrusting himself into the public spotlight, Donald trump differentiated himself from all other business leaders of his time. Caution and shyness were not part of his DNA. He firmly believed that that the burnishing of his ego was critical to his business success."

"Most business figures have peanut-size egos – or if they have large egos, they are eager to conceal them, believing that the very act of parading themselves in public is a flamboyance that might prove bad for business; they also feel that self-glorification is a sin that only distracts from the selling of the company's product. In stark contrast, Donald Trump believes firmly in a nexus of the forging of his ego – his image – and his success in business.

"To initially forge his ego, he felt he had to open up to the world, to nurture a persona that was of interest to the public. In doing so, he had to reveal himself in a way that other business figures rarely did. He had to reveal a good deal of his life-style to the public, be accessible to the media, and deliver colorful yet pithy quotes.

"Other business leaders exhibited much restraint in their public statements, not wanting to cause even the slightest discomfort to shareholders. Trump with less than 1 percent of his net worth tied up in a public company (which controlled his casino hotels), had no such concerns, openly calling people idiots, and, worse, cursing routinely, exhibiting bouts of anger and fire and passion, making fun of himself.

"If most of his business colleagues wanted to avoid the public spotlight, Donald Trump seemed to be perfectly comfortable in it.
...
"His most novel business lessons are those that encourage executives to burnish their egos and trumpet their achievements in public; these are not lessons that most business leaders will find easy to adopt. But they have worked for Donald Trump.
...
"It is Trump's unabashed willingness to be so public a figure that makes him unique on the business landscape. ... By watching Trump in action and under-standing the way he turns the quest for publicity and the nurturing of his personal brand into successful business strategies, other business leaders might become a little more willing to make the media and other means of communication work for them in a positive way."

26. "He takes chances where other people wouldn't; and I think people are fascinated by that."

27. "He's so atypical. He does things that are counter cultural. Most of us middle-class Americans are taught not to brag about money and to keep our chins down. Donald walks around with his chin up; and he brags about money all the time. You always think he's giggling about it and that he's in on the joke. That's why he's gotten away with it for so long."

28. "In the late 1980's, a major business magazine did a story saying that everything Trump touched turned to gold. 'I started to believe that.' He began to think that he could leave others to run his various businesses and go off and have a good time. The whole exercise was fun while it lasted: 'I was going to Paris to the fashion shows, for the girls, not for the fashions. I was doing things that were wild and good and cool and fun.'"

"As Trump stepped up his purchasing of businesses and baubles, he chose not to worry what might happen to him if storm clouds appeared. So confident in his own business skills was he that he left the daily operations of his businesses to subordinates."

"... On one occasion, while in Paris, he allowed his subordinates to handle a big lease. It never got signed. At the time, their failure to close the deal did not bother him that much. He figured he would get the lease when he got back. Later when things turned bad, he remembered that incident all too vividly as the classic example of how he had screwed up, of how he had not kept on top of things, and how he had paid a very heavy price. 'If I had been there, there's no way they wouldn't have signed the lease. But I wasn't there.'"

"In later years when he analyzed what had gone wrong, he put it all down to losing focus. When he kept his focus, he did well – simple as that. The cynics attributed his business acumen riding good markets, but Trump thought differently. 'I always made money in down markets. I made a lot of money in the early '80's and the very early part of the 90's. I wasn't nearly as focused as I am now in 2004 or as I was before.'"

"Why had he allowed himself to lose focus?"

"First, he was overly competitive. He wanted to win.

"Second, he got bored too quickly.

"He lost patience with the deals that he made. His solution was to search for more deals. To others, such behavior smacked of avarice, but not to Trump. He was built not to savor the asset, but to enjoy the struggle for the asset – and that meant he had to strike and then move on. 'For me, you see, the important thing is the getting ... not the having,' he wrote in his 1990 book, *Trump: Surviving at the Top*."

29. "Donald's needs and tastes, were simple almost Spartan – steak or hamburger for dinner maybe a simple pasta dish with a diet cola that he drank from a straw for fear of disease. For all his possessions it seemed that there were none that he ever had the time or peace of mind to enjoy. ... John [Trump's middle name] won't have [any] time for anything outside business and rarely beyond the issue of the moment. He cares nothing for art, music and books. He has no hobbies nor diversions, not even a passing interest in

gambling and the games that made him so much money. Even sports failed to interest him, except for boxing, which he loved."

30. "He clearly resented what he considered the "charity" game, and he said so in *The Art of the Deal*: 'I don't kid myself about why I asked to speak at four chairs so many events,' he complained. 'It's not because I'm such a great guy. The reason is that people who run charities know that I've got wealthy friends and can get them to buy tables. I understand the game, and while I don't like to play it, there is no graceful way out.'"

31. "Donald was simply unable to cope with the emotional demands that the crash [the helicopter accident that killed his three high-level executives of his three casinos in Atlantic City] placed on him. I wondered whether he cared about anyone other than himself, or if he [expressed] sincere emotion."

"I learned from those who made the rounds with him the night of the crash that Donald was terribly uncomfortable and emotionally detached when he visited the families of their homes. But the whole night he had a look of fear in his eyes. He kept saying over and over, 'I can't believe these guys are dead. This is impossible. They can't be.' The fear was for himself. He had lost his two key players: Mark, the one who showcased the Trump name so well, the promoter who was instrumental in enhancing the Trump image; and Steve, the manager and operator, the one who kept all the pieces together and protected Donald from his own worst excesses."

"Still, with all of his troubles, there's something very disarming about Donald Trump, and he possesses both courage and daring. Like him or not, the man is an original, determined to survive at the top."

32. "[The] ['schizophrenia of our {elite} culture']: You're supposed to make money but not be a braggart. You're supposed to be modest. Donald Trump breaks that mold. He flaunts his success. That makes him very attractive. He doesn't apologize for his success."

UNFAVORABLE PERSPECTIVES

1. "In many ways [Donald was] a Jekyll and Hyde guy. He could be enormously charming and you'd almost think, 'Gee, this is a nice, decent, warm guy, and then the bad twin would come out.'"

2. "If you spend any time with him, you see that he's always pumping himself up, always. He really believes he's the smartest, the best-looking, the best lay."

3. "He can be mean and nasty and he has horrible attitudes about women. But he really believes in himself. He has this gut thing, where he goes ahead on his own gas. And it's why he's a successful entrepreneur."

4. "Trump struck me as adolescent, hilariously ostentatious, arbitrary, unkind, profane, dishonest, loudly opinionated, and consistently wrong. He remains the most vain man I have ever met. And he was trying to make a good impression."

5. "He was fearsome. Everyone was afraid of his tirades and his power to get things in the press to influence him."

6. "There is something about him that's very juvenile. It's hard to believe he's a grown up person who went to college. ... He's like a kid, and he's got that brash narcissistic thing that works for him. He has an enormous appeal to the masses because of that. ... He once threatened to buy the Daily News so he could have me fired. And, yes, I still go on liking him, no matter what you or I think about him case-wise."

7. "He's the greatest manipulator of the media there is. – He's got a very fertile and creative imagination about how to spin issues, and he's brilliant at turning lemons into lemonade. In everything that fails he spins into a victory."

8. "Lying is second nature to him. More than anyone else I have ever met, Trump has the ability to convince himself that whatever he is saying at any given moment is true, or sort of true, or at least *ought* to be true."

9. "He's just pathological. He lies and lies and lies."

10. "When Donald declares that people are saying '[W]hat a great deal he made on the Plaza,' [*Interviewer*: 'No, they're not.' ... "You never say, 'I made mistakes. Gee, I'm in trouble. Things are bad.'] Donald: 'Everyone makes mistakes.' [*Interviewer*: 'You haven't said it.'] Donald: 'I make mistakes.'"

11. "Donald is a believer in the big-lie theory. If you say something again and again, people will believe you. He was always a phony, and we filled our papers with him."

12. "Donald's style when it comes to the truth is creative and very much a part of who he is. He's a carnival barker. He's a B.T. Barnum. The truth is for university ethics professors."

13. "In giving a name to his lack of truth-telling, it's as if Trump feels pride in expanding on the truth. He finds nothing wrong with the practice, he is simply playing up to people's fantasies."

14. "Those who do their research on any or all of Trump's statements find a good part of them to be true, but a certain part to be exaggerated. While journalists pick apart some of these statements, Trump goes ballistic. When he engages in truthful hyperbole, he seems playful; but when someone challenges him on such hyperbole, he is anything but playful."

15. "He lied about the membership fee for one of his golf courses, inflating the figure by $100,000. He lied about the extent of his debt in the early 90s to make his climb back to solvency look more heroic."

16. "Trump also made a number of unsubstantiated claims in an attempt to slander and discredit O'Brien including a made-up claim that the writer was once arrested for stalking. 'I guess that was probably taken off the Internet,' Trump admitted.'"

17. "A very clear and visible side effect of my lawyers' questioning of Trump is that he [was revealed as] a routine and habitual fabulist [a liar, especially a person who invents elaborate, dishonest stories]."

18. "Trump is unique [because of his] blatant self-promotion and his almost comical use of hyperbole, making an art form out of bragging."

19. "He is, above all else, incurably addicted to self-glorifying publicity."

20. "He was a mommy's boy, and terribly spoiled as a child. He had everything he wanted and never had much taken away from him. I came across the embryonic Donald Trump: In their school days, usually, people lose that trace of saying I want that; 'Give it to me, or I will smash you.' He has not lost that trait."

21. "Donald is very thin-skinned. He takes everything personally. Everything."

22. "He was still Trump, still the cocky, blunt kid from Queens, still the guy who would say what others only thought."

23. "At the age of eight, little Donald borrowed Robert's [his brother] cherished toy blocks, glued them together into one giant skyscraper and never returned them, thereafter exercising his fantasies about changing Manhattan's skyline."

24. "To disagree with Trump is to be wrong. To portray Trump in a way that does not fit with his image of himself is to be a loser. It is an approach to life that may work in business (where Trump can walk out and not deal with people who displease him), but government leaders do not enjoy that luxury, especially the president of the United States."

25. "Trump has often boasted (in the past and on the campaign trail) that he buys the friendship of politicians so they 'do what I want.'"

26. "Sixteen pages of *Think Big* are devoted to revenge. All of them run directly contrary to this basic biblical teaching. Trump leaves no room for doubt that revenge is a guiding principle of his life – 'My motto is: Always get even.'"

27. "Erecting gaudy buildings did not bring Donald Trump the national attention he craved. It was football that made him famous. Hiring a new

general manager for his real estate firm drew little media attention, but 'I hire a coach for a football team and there are sixty or seventy reporters calling to interview me.' Trump's foray into professional football provides an early example of a business career built on breaking, ignoring, or making up rules."

28. "For all his dealings with Trump, Sullivan was repeatedly astonished by the businessman's lack of prudence. He said that whenever Trump saw an opportunity to collect more money or to cut his costs by not paying people what they had earned, he did. 'Common sense just never took hold when Trump had money on his mind,' Sullivan told me several times."

29. "Donald no doubt enjoys the bridge player's definition of trump: a winning play by a card that outranks all others. But other definitions include "a thing of small value, a trifle" and "to deceive or cheat" as well as 'to blow or sound a trumpet.' As a verb, trump means 'to devise in an unscrupulous way' and 'to forge, fabricate or invent,' as in 'trumped-up' charges. Donald'"

30. "Trump distorts information, contradicts himself, and blocks inquiries into his conduct by journalists, law enforcement, business regulators, and other people's lawyers. Again, the record shows decades of Trump's skill in pursuing this strategy successfully."

31. "This is a man who started his [presidential] campaign by saying wages are too high. This is a man who, when he does construction projects, deals with mob-controlled unions. That's why Trump Towers [in Manhattan] are concrete, because the steelworkers are an honest union. This is a man who cheats workers out of their pay. Four dollars an hour he paid, and he cheated them out of some of their pay. That's what a judge found. This is a man who tells vendors, Do this work. They do it and then he says, I am not going to pay you."

32. "[This is a man]" ... who has never demonstrated any interest in anyone or anything but himself and his own enrichment; who insults veterans, threatens a free press, mocks the handicapped, denigrates women, immigrants and all Muslims; a man who took more than a day to remember to disavow a supporter who advocates white supremacy and the Ku Klux Klan; an infantile, bullying man who, depending on his mood, is willing to discard old and established alliances, treaties and long-standing relationships."

33. "I don't know if you saw the piece the other day where the manager, or whoever was responsible as his witness, at the Doral [Miami], over this guy who didn't get paid the last $34,000 for his paint – he was a Benjamin Moore paint dealer – testified Mr. Trump felt he had paid enough. Nobody runs their business on that basis. You can think, and with good reason, of all sorts of bad

things that corporations do. But they don't go around saying to vendors or workers, "Uh, we paid enough. We're not going to pay you."

34. "Donald also learned a lot from Roy Cohn [New York City mob lawyer and Sen. Joseph McCarthy's assistant in the 1950s anti-communist witch hunts] about how to create a falsehood. Like when the government went after Trump and his dad for discriminating against blacks and Puerto Ricans, and they said, 'This was an effort to put people on welfare in our buildings.' No, it wasn't. The [government's] housing testers who were sent were black and Hispanic people who were economically qualified and they were turned away and then white people showed up with the exact same economics and they were shown multiple apartments."

35. "Always go on the attack. Always accuse the other side of dishonesty. And be ruthless. Remember one of the reasons he loved Roy Cohn – I quote him in the book – whom he regarded as not just as a mentor but as a second father, was he said Roy would brutalize for you. That's the lesson. Listen, for Donald's entire life he has broken the rules or ignored the rules and it's done well for him. So why would you behave any other way? If you were raised in the household where your parents told you be immoral, and you got away with it, well, of course you'd be immoral."

36. "He's not any different than when I met him, when he was in his early 40s. Donald is a guy who has no empathy for other people, who doesn't see other people as human beings. He sees them as things to be used. That's why when he was challenged about cutting off health care for his sickly grandnephew, over money, and he was asked, as I report in the book, 'Don't you think that will look cold-hearted?' [He replied] 'What else can I do?' There is no moral core inside Donald Trump. There is no moral compass. It doesn't exist."

37. "His skill at shutting down law enforcement investigations – I cite those four grand juries, etc. – is extraordinary. He knows when to run to the cops and rat out people, or tell them information that will help them. He knows how to use the court system to cover up what he's done by making a settlement on the condition that the record be sealed. And he's masterful at this. It's just astonishing how masterful he is at it."

38. "And then he's masterful at the conventions of journalism. All journalists who keep their jobs accurately, quote what people tell them. Most journalists, even at the best papers, they don't have a deep understanding of the things that they are reporting on. I can show you people at the New York Times, the L.A. Times, the Wall Street Journal, who really know their stuff. But I can also show you a lot of them who don't and have pretty superficial knowledge of what they're doing. Donald avoids group A and he goes for group B."

39. "Donald is not a good negotiator. He's not a good businessman. And he often overplays his hand because of hubris. What he does when that happens is that he threatens to make terrible trouble for people with litigation, to tie them all up, so what they'll do is settle with him, because who wants to spend – as one brave guy in the demolition workers did – spend 18 years in litigation with Trump. You just want it to go away. And he knows that. And he uses it. And if you don't have the money to pursue him for 18 years, you have to have a lawyer who's really willing to do that, you're going to be told by the lawyers, there's no gain here. And he knows that."

40. "People who are in economic terror – that's about half the population – Donald Trump poses as a savior. 'I will save you.' 'Only I can save you.' And to people who have been abandoned by both parties, they've been actively worked against by both parties, that's a powerful message."

41. "He had no patience for civilities if he saw no business purpose to them. 'Forgetting' the average person was a cornerstone of Donald's philosophy."

42. "Donald had what he always wanted in any potential deal, an adversary."

43. "His hubris was practically boundless."

44. "I had learned that Donald never tipped anyone, not waiters, waitresses, doormen, bellhops, not even his drivers. He never gave it a thought. Like other very wealthy people, it seems he never carried any money. He used to laugh about it."

45. "It was an odd contradiction, one I believe he never quite understood himself: how he could be so intensely concerned about what the public thought of him, yet care so little about their sensibilities. The fact that they were guests at his hotels and players at his tables seem to be nothing to him."

46. "The tales of his erratic behavior, his lack of operational knowledge and his explosive temper were all too prevalent in the industry by now."

47. "That [Trump's publicly exploiting his extra-marital affair] taught me, if I didn't know already, that Donald was so self-centered and unfeeling that he put his business ahead of everything else. His children, especially his eldest son, Donny, Jr., were devastated. But there was a business advantage to be gained, or so he thought, and he continued to publicly promote his [extra-marital] affair. His family, it seemed, was expendable. He went on record describing Marla as 'better than at 10.' 'Denigrating the competition,' as he described the deal-maker's art, he attacked his wife as 'arrogant' and 'another Leona Helmsley' (the hotel queen he previously described as 'a vicious, horrible woman' and 'a disgrace to humanity'). – Sloshed around in the press as it was, the spectacle severely damaged Donald's image. Suddenly he looked like an ogre, emotionally abusive, self-centered, the money-grabber

squabbling over a 25 million settlement with his wife, a mere 1 or 2 percent of his perceived billions."

48. "His patience was even shorter than his attention span."

49. "As he has run his empire and ascended as a mega star on reality TV, Trump has often been accused of being a bully, which he denies. He does, however, acknowledge being a 'very assertive, aggressive kid.'"

50. "Life with Trump is a roller coaster of anticlimaxes."

51. "It takes a certain kind of intelligence to spin a yarn so counterintuitive and defiantly false that some people will believe it anyway. Alternatively, Trump could be just as confused as he hopes others will be."

52. "When Trump isn't playing king, he's happy to be the court jester. With a shrug of his shoulders and a smirkish smile, he conveys 'whatever.'

53. "Whenever Trump saw an opportunity to collect more money or to cut his costs by not paying people what they had earned, he did."

54. "Judge _____ ruled that Trump had engaged in a conspiracy to cheat the workers of their pay."

55. [Trump:] "At Trump University, we teach success," Trump said, looking into the camera in a 2005 promotional video. 'That's what it's all about – success. It's going to happen to you. We're going to have professors and adjunct professors that are absolutely terrific – terrific people, terrific brains, successful. We are going to have the best of the best. These are all people that are handpicked by me.'

"None of those statements were true.

"The faux university also did not have professors, not even part-time adjunct professors, and the 'faculty' (as they were called) were certainly not 'the best of the best.' They were commissioned sales people, many with no experience in real estate. One managed a fast-food joint, as Senator Marco Rubio would point out during the March 3 Republican primary debate in 2016. Two other instructors were in personal bankruptcy while collecting fees from would-be Trump University graduates eager to learn how to get rich."

56. [From a woman candidate on Trump's TV reality show, *The Apprentice*] "As Trump closes in on the Republican nomination, I'm constantly asked about the man and his campaign. I even wrote a book on the topic, *Decoding the Donald*. Since last summer, I've watched Trump mount his incendiary campaign for the presidency – full of quixotic promises, bombastic rhetoric and petulant personal attacks – and memories of my time in Trump's TV universe resurface. ...

"The premise of his show was more or less the pitch he's making to America: Trump is the boss, and he'll hire the best people. We were supposedly competing to be mini-entrepreneurs, team leaders, junior managers executing their ideas in a business empire. This wasn't quite what the show rewarded, though. What it largely rewarded was giving attention to Donald Trump. ...

"We were deferential and solicitous; time and again, I was prompted to repeat the fawning platitudes that had gotten me on the show. Cameras followed my every move while producers whispered in my ear, keeping me wrapped up in this distorted reality. ...

"This isn't to say Trump wasn't charming. Just as he effectively uses humor at his rallies, Trump regaled us with jokes – kidding us about the budding romance between contestants, or unexpectedly dropping a "fo' shizzle" when announcing that our reward one week was to rap with Snoop Dogg. Maybe it was just the charm of a rascal who just doesn't operate with a filter. Maybe it was all an act. Either way, Trump had a charisma that could balance out his crass tendency to say or do things that other people's conscience or sense of decency would never allow. ...

"The Donald Trump I saw up close is very much the same man who alternately captivates and revolts America. As a candidate, he's been uniquely attuned to poll numbers, turning them into a talking point in a way no candidate had imagined before. ...

"On the trail, even if he can't get the rest of the world to call him "Mr. Trump," his deep personal insecurities have given him a real political advantage: He knows how to capitalize on others' insecurities. ...

"Want to throw off an opponent? Do something out of bounds, like attacking their spouse's appearance. Want to embarrass a boyish 22-year-old *Apprentice* candidate who lacks your machismo? Sit in your boardroom, cameras rolling, and ask him if he's a virgin. Want to win white working-class voters in the midst of an existential crisis? Attack immigrants, advocate a border wall, and promise to bring those would-be supporters back to a simpler time of cultural and economic supremacy. ...

"Today, when I watch the rallies and the friendly TV appearances, I get the distinct sense that the line between Trumpland and actual reality is blurring. Donald Trump has turned the campaign into a reality show, and we can't seem to stop watching. Having lived in the former, I can attest that's not a good thing."

57. "From his days peddling the false notion that former President Barack Obama was born in Kenya, to his inflated claims about how many people attended his inaugural, to his description just last week of receiving two phone

calls – one from the president of Mexico and another from the head of the Boy Scouts – that never happened, Mr. Trump is trafficking in hyperbole, distortion and fabrication on practically a daily basis. ...

"The glaring difference between Mr. Trump and his predecessors is the sheer magnitude of falsehoods and exaggerations; PolitiFact rates just 20 percent of the statements it reviewed as true, and a total of 69 percent either mostly false, false or "Pants on Fire." That leaves scholars like Ms. Goodwin to wonder whether Mr. Trump, in elevating the art of political fabrication, has forever changed what Americans are willing to tolerate from their leaders."

58. "The big concern as relates to Trump as President would be his strongman type of personality coupled with a cult of personality worship amongst his followers. This worship is something that Trump himself is well aware of, and it makes him all the more dangerous."

59. "He lacks diplomacy – on purpose."

60. "He could never be old money," He could never be the kind of people who were into museums and art and opera, things like that. He could never, ever be that. And he wanted it, and he resented it, and then he played upon it – and then he said, 'Oh, I'm better than that, my elite is better than the old elite.'

61. "Trump is a tiny little boy, knocking on a big mahogany door, saying, 'Let me in!' [to the door of cultural elitism] And he's never going to get in. And I think the ultimate irony of his life is he has been elevated to the most powerful job in the world. And so long as he is in it, it declines in importance." He likened it to Greek tragedy. 'There is no bigger job'. There is no greater way for him to do it. And there is no greater proof that he is a pretender."

62. "He has embraced the notion of a populist revolution without renouncing a single trapping of his gold-plated lifestyle. Can he really run as the elite instead of against the elite?"

MODERATE PERSPECTIVES

His Children

1. [On Donald Trump Jr.'s view of his father at age 12] "How can you say you love us? You don't love us! You don't even love yourself. You just love your money."

2. [On what it was like to grow up as Donald Trump's child – Donald Trump Jr.] "It wasn't a typical 'let's go play catch in the backyard' sort of father-son relationship. We always went to job sites with him. We'd be in his office playing with trucks as a six-year-old while he's negotiating deals with presidents of major companies."

3. [Donald Trump Jr., discussing the years he lived with his mother, Ivana Trump, after his parents' divorce. ("He says this without a trace of bitterness.")] "My father is a very hardworking guy, and that's his focus in life, so I got a lot of the paternal attention that a boy wants and needs from my grandfather."

4. [On what it was like to grow up as Donald Trump's child, Eric Trump] "In a way, [my brother, Donald Jr.] raised me. My father, I love and I appreciate, but he always worked 24 hours a day."

5. [On his father's competitiveness, according to his son, Eric Trump:] "He would try to push me over, just so he could beat his 10-year-old son down the mountain."

6. [On his competitiveness, according to Trump's daughter, Ivanka] "We were sort of bred to be competitive. Dad encourages it. I remember skiing with him and we were racing. I was ahead, and he reached his ski pole out and pulled me back."

7. "The greatest thing that has come out of *The Apprentice*, being a family member [Donald Trump Junior], is that America sees Donald trump as a human. He's not a Ken Lay [former chairman and CEO of Enron] or this horrible corporate guy that goes back to his cave at night. He's a person. He's a smart-ass. He can come back really quickly. He's a funny guy. He's not some android. As his son, the greatest thing for me is to see that people get to see that he's a great guy – fun-loving, humorous guy – he still works, but he's not just this stiff who sits there and says, 'Okay, you're fired – next.'"

MALICIOUS PERSPECTIVES

Donald Trump as a Possible "Pathic" (sociopath, psychopath, narcipath, malignant narcissist)

[Selections from internet articles]

Trump as a possible extreme narcipath

1. "Is Donald Trump a textbook narcissist?" - The Washington Post
2. "Donald Trump's Narcissism" - CNN.com
3. "Is Donald Trump a malignant narcissist?" - Quora
4. "We should stop calling Trump a narcissist" –The Hill

Trump as a possible sociopath

1. "Beck: Trump's a sociopath, When has he 'Truly felt for someone'" – Mediaite
2. "Trump & Questions about Sociopathy and Narcissism" - Psychology
3. "Robert Reich Accuses Donald Trump Of Behaving Like a Sociopath" – Fortune

Trump as a possible psychopath

1. "Oliver Calls Trump A 'Toddler Psychopath'"–Townhall
2. "The BBC's New Media editor Called Donald Trump A 'Psychopath'"– Heatstreet

THE AUTHOR'S COMMENTS REGARDING THE SEVERITY OF THESE MALICIOUS PERSPECTIVES

To be sure, the quotations in Part One of this book by Mr. Trump obviously reveal and expose his character, though hardly his personality, and its public persona, as he states his points of view in public, in interviews, in the media, in private, and in his books. He certainly belongs with those individuals termed "ruthless opportunists"; but with style and flair, to put it politely. Yet, as for his being a deliberately malicious malcontent out to do everyone harm for his own purpose and delight, well, that requires some analysis to the contrary.

As for my own estimation of his character, I do not consider Donald Trump as *innately*, predominantly, evil or mean-spirited, a predator, a psychopath, or sociopath, nor narcipath – malignant narcissist – (each, in its own way, bent on even breaking down, destroying, the well-being, the life, of others if his own well-being is threatened in any way, unjustly or even justly), as some writers (on the internet) imply; but is rather as basically a *hard-wired*, hard-natured person; who prefers, in one way or another, conflict rather than harmony, strife rather than love, war rather than peace. Contrarily, I cannot imagine him as a "bleeding heart", a kindly soul, a fair-minded, peace-loving, compassionate, considerate, sensitive person – in the main: a man of integrity and sensitivity. Generous, yes, for a planned purpose, to only those loyal to him, and *only* to him, *at all times, in all situations*. The truth for him is *his own* truth, or otherwise stated, half-truths; his outspoken honesty, on which he prides himself, is a *calculated* honesty, that follows the so-called maxim: "Honesty is the best policy" – yes, as the best way to "rope in" clients, customers, the gullible, the ignorant, the "suckers" – rather than, a *moral* honesty. For him, 'might is right', not its converse, 'right is might'. – "Don't you dare tell me what's right no matter what you've heard otherwise." He himself proudly claims that he loves beautiful women; yes, as an aphrodisiac; who, his having once climaxed (both physically and psychologically), to be discarded or used. He's smarter (wiser?) than anyone else; after all, who has accumulated, "by the book", so many millions of dollars and such innumerable women with such flair and style, and who has gotten away with it. True; to give him that credit; but smarter than whom? To what class does he refer by "anyone else"? Answer: *the lower denominator of humankind, the humanness*, (our ego-sensuality-self) of human nature, psychology, as all that which weighs predominantly on our race, I grant – our ego-sensuality, in sum; yet, what of moral, spiritual, scientific, philosophic, contemplative, individuals whose basic nature strives for *transcendence* through *integrity*: justice, wisdom, peace, love, understanding, sensitivity, brotherhood, simplicity; who struggle against ignorance, injustice, who keep the world of man mostly balanced, protective, against inhumanity, who sooner or later take to task the injustice and ignorance, the greed and tyranny of the autocratic, despotic, type wherever they're found in human relationships.

Yes, Trump is outspoken to a "T"; which is an admirable trait, often a courageous trait, (he *says* what others only *think*; and so, he opens the way for more forwardness, more "telling it like it is") : an *abrasive forthrightness*. But what of *sensitive* forthrightness? Do we slap a person, twist his arm, demean, reproach him/her, with the truth; or do we *sensitively* approach a person with the truth – even a white lie? Does Mr. Trump make this distinction? Not that I can tell, unless it is in his favor to do so – if he even *can* do so.

From all this analysis, in sum, then, as for my own estimation of Trump's character, being hard-natured, such as he is, does not mean that his range of psycho-physical <u>temperament</u> and intelligence extends to the abnormal extremes of the pathology of the psychopath, sociopath, or narcipath (malignant narcissist) – *pathics* in a collective name; even though he may harbor minimal traits of each of these conditions. In which case, he would more likely than not be excluded from those of a natural-born pathic nature.

Trump's psychological life would not be innately dominated by either one nor more of these pathic inclinational and behavioral patterns. Rather, his foremost focus would be wired to enact and achieve his goals moderately, securely, criminally, deceitfully, rather than being overtly, dominantly, governed by his particular pathic-tendencies – those which inhere in inhuman monsters, as Stalin, for one; Pol Pot, for another; Idi Amin, for still another).

True, Trump could (and has) easily enough ruin a person's life (in good part by legal suits, or false accusations made public); but not so easily by violently killing or torturing others, if necessary; such acts would destroy, if not his hard-natured conscience, then his reputation, his honor, his heroic status. Not so, the innate pathic, who would not stop short of guilt nor remorse, nor fear, nor loss of reputation, in violently eliminating a threat to his way of life.*

Which leads me to Part Three of this book as an intermediary transition between Trump the psychological man and Trump the so-called mythological man. This part includes (1) pertinent selections related to Trump from the 1914 novel, *The Titan*, by Theodore Dreiser, (2) pertinent selections from Shakespeare' plays, and (3) fictional impressions by this author that interpret a rapid flow of Trump's likely impressionistic thoughts both human and trans-human.

---

*For a more in-depth study of the pathic nature, told mostly by their victims, I recommend my PDF Book; *Of Pathics and Evil: a Philosophy against Malice*, available by email contact, thepublicbenefit1@gmail.com

PART THREE

Fictional Impressions of Trump's Character and
Tactics Stated by
Theodore Dreiser, Shakespeare, and by this Author

Fictional Impressions of Trump's Likely 'All-too-human' Persona

*The selections I include in **Part Three** present three fictional portrayals in reference to, Donald Trump's psychological persona transitioning to **Part Four** which focuses on the question whether or not Trump is transcendently an overman in the German philosopher, Nietzsche's meaning of the concept, Übermensch. In other words, he may be a supreme man-of-affairs, but is he a supreme overman-of-affairs, such that he has attained a kind of balance between his humanness and his transcendence that benefits not only himself, but, as a political **statesman**, in favor of man's continuing ascendancy of justice and wisdom over injustice and ignorance?*

I

TRUMP'S HUMANNESS AS A SUPREME EGO-SENSUALIST

A Fictional Likeness

Theodore Dreiser

[Selections from the novel *The Titan*] This author somehow struck an astonishing psychological likeness between the main character, Frank Algernon Cowperwood, and Trump's overall character in this 1914 novel, *The Titan*. I include these passages so that the reader may glean a kind of stream of consciousness of the landscape of Trump's mindset through this fictional character. Perhaps not very likely, but It's almost as if Donald Trump read this book, and decided to model himself after the main character, Frank Cowperwood.

1. Frank Algernon Cowperwood does not believe in the people; He does not trust them. To him they constitute no more than a field upon which corn is to be sown, and from which it is to be reaped. They present but a mass of bent backs, their knees and faces in the mire, over which as over a floor he strides to superiority. His private and inmost faith is in himself alone.

2. He did not believe in either the strength of the masses or their ultimate rights, though he sympathized with the condition of individuals, and did believe that men like himself were sent into the world to better perfect its

mechanism and habitable order. ... They could not be expected to understand his dreams or his visions, or to share in the magnificence and social dominance which he craved.

3. His thoughts as to life and control had given him a fixed policy. He could, should, and would rule alone. No man must ever again have the least claim on him save that of supplicant. By right of financial intellect and courage he was first and would so prove it. Men must swing around him as planets around the sun.

4. Cowperwood was now entering upon a great public career ... raw, glittering force, however, compounded of the cruel Machiavellianism of nature, if it is to be but Machiavellian, seems to exercise a profound attraction for the conventionality rooted. Your cautious citizen of average means, looking out through the eye of his dull world of seeming fact, is often the first to forgive or condone the grim butcheries of theory by which the strong rise.

5. Seeing the manner in which he had managed to wrest victory out of defeat, these gentlemen had experienced a change of heart and announced that they would now gladly help finance any new enterprise which Cowperwood would might undertake. ... In the commercial heart of this world Frank Algernon Cowperwood had truly become a figure of giant significance. How wonderful it is that men grow until, like colossus is, they bestride the world, or, like banyan trees, they drop roots from every branch and are themselves a forest. ... His properties were like a net – the parasite goldthread – linked together as they were and draining two of the three important sides of the city.

6. The humdrum conventional world could not brook his daring, his insouciance, his constant desire to call a spade a spade, his genial sufficiency was taunt and a mockery to many. The hard implication of his eye was driven by the weaker as fire is feared by burned child.

7. It is curious how that first and most potent tendency of the human mind, ambition, becomes finally dominating. Here was Cowperwood, rich beyond the wildest dreams of the average man, celebrated in a local and in some respects a national way, who was nevertheless feeling that by no means had his true aims been achieved. ... he was not yet looked upon as some money prince. He could not rank as yet with the magnets of the East – the Sequoias of Wall Street. Until he could stand with these men, acknowledged as such by all. ... what did it avail?

8. And this giant himself, rushing on to new struggles and new difficulties in an older land, forever separating the goad of a restless heart – for him was no ultimate peace, no real understanding, but only hunger and thirst and wonder.

9. The race is to the swift, he said to himself over and over. Yes, and the battle is to the strong. He would test whether the world would trample him under foot or no.

10. "I satisfy myself" [compare Trump's own statement] was his private law, but so to do he must assuage and control the prejudices of other men.

11. *If through luck and effort he became sufficiently powerful financially he might then hope to dictate to society. Individualistic and even anarchistic in character, and without a shred of true democracy, yet temperamentally he was in sympathy with the mass more than he was with the class, and he understood the mass better.* [My italics, in order to emphasize Trump's possible long-time intention to run for, and his personal attitude toward, the United States' Presidency]

12. Sex interest in all strong men usually endures unto the end, governed sometimes by a stoic resignation. The experiment of such attraction can, as they well know, be made over and over, but to what end? For many it becomes too troublesome.

13. Roughly speaking, it might have been said of him that youth and hope in women—particularly youth when combined with beauty and ambition in a girl—touched him. He responded keenly to her impulse to do or be something in this world, whatever it might be, and he looked on the smart, egoistic vanity of so many with a kindly, tolerant, almost parental eye. Poor little organisms growing on the tree of life – they would burn out and fade soon enough. He did not know the ballad of the roses of yesteryear, but if he had it would have appealed to him. He did not care to rifle them, willy-nilly; but should their temperaments or tastes incline them in his direction, they would not suffer vastly in their lives because of him. The fact was, the man was essentially generous where women were concerned. ... As a matter of fact, in most cases he was as much sinned against as sinning, since the provocation was as much offered as given.

14. The difficulty with this situation, as with all such where an individual ventures thus bucaneeringly on the sea of sex, is the possibility of those storms which result from misplaced confidence, and from our built-up system of ethics relating to property in women. To Cowperwood, however, who was a law unto himself, who knew no law except such as might be imposed upon him by his lack of ability to think, this possibility of entanglement, wrath, rage, pain, offered no particular obstacle. It was not at all certain that any such thing would follow. Where the average man might have found one such liaison difficult to manage, Cowperwood, as we have seen, had previously entered on several such affairs almost simultaneously; and now he had ventured on yet another; in the last instance with much greater feeling and enthusiasm. The previous affairs had been emotional makeshifts at best—more or less idle

philanderings in which his deeper moods and feelings were not concerned. In the case of Mrs. Sohlberg all this was changed. For the present at least she was really all in all to him. But this temperamental characteristic of his relating to his love of women, his artistic if not emotional subjection to their beauty, and the mystery of their personalities led him into still a further affair. ... At last he saw clearly, as within a chalice-like nimbus, that the ultimate end of fame, power, vigor was beauty, and that beauty was a compound of the taste, the emotion, the innate culture, passion, and dreams of a woman like Berenice Fleming.

15. Truth to say, he must always have youth, the illusion of beauty, vanity in womanhood, the novelty of a new, untested temperament, quite as he must have pictures, old porcelain, music, a mansion, illuminated missals, power, the applause of the great, unthinking world. As has been said, this promiscuous attitude on Cowperwood's part was the natural flowering out of a temperament that was chronically promiscuous, intellectually uncertain, and philosophically anarchistic. From one point of view it might have been said of him that he was seeking the realization of an ideal, yet to one's amazement our very ideals change at times and leave us floundering in the dark. What is an ideal, anyhow? A wraith, a mist, a perfume in the wind, a dream of fair water. The soul-yearning of a girl like Antoinette Nowak was a little too strained for him. It was too ardent, too clinging, and he had gradually extricated himself, not without difficulty, from that particular entanglement. Since then he had been intimate with other women for brief periods, but to no great satisfaction – Dorothy Ormsby, Jessie Belle Hinsdale, Toma Lewis, Hilda Jewell; but they shall be names merely.

16. Cowperwood detected that pliability of intellect which, while it might spell disaster to some, spelled success for him. He wanted the intellectual servants. He was willing to pay them handsomely, to keep them busy, to treat them with almost princely courtesy, but he must have the utmost loyalty. Stimson, while maintaining his calm and reserve, could have kissed the arch-episcopal hand. Such is the subtlety of contact.

17. "I like lawsuits. We'll tie them up so that they'll beg for quarter." His eyes twinkled cheerfully.

18. It is one of the splendid yet sinister fascinations of life that there is no tracing to their ultimate sources all the winds of influence that play upon a given barque [bark]—all the breaths of chance that fill or desert our bellied or our sagging sails. We plan and plan, but who by taking thought can add a cubit to his stature? Who can overcome or even assist the Providence that shapes our ends, rough hew them as we may.

19. Who plans the steps that lead lives on to splendid glories, or twist them into narrow sacrifices, Or make them dark, disdainful, contentious tragedies? The soul within? And whence comes it? Of God? [T]hat instinct for the essential and vital which invariably possessed him.

20. Rushing like a great comet to the zenith, his path a blazing trail, Frank Cowperwood did for the hour the terrors and wonders of individuality. But for him also the eternal equation – the pathos of the discovery that even Giants are but pygmies, and that *an ultimate balance must be struck* [this author's italics].

II

TRUMP'S HUMANNESS AS A SUPREME DECEITIST

These related passages, selected from Shakespeare's plays are intended to define, Mr. Trump as suspect to his intimidating beliefs, and values. They are so incredibly insightful for their poetic veracity in applying not only to Trump, but to his type of person, as he and others present themselves, overtly and covertly. Some passages, I know, are in the extreme; yet, how far would Trump go in the extreme, if only to save face?!
Accordingly, there is no way I can omit these in this Trump study.

1.
Rude am I in my speech, And little blessed with the soft phrase of peace.

2.
Let me have men about me that are fat,
... Sleek-headed men and such as sleep a-nights.

3.
Stars, hide your fires;
Let not light see my black and deep desires.

4.
Cry havoc and let slip the dogs of war!

5.
But are not some whole that we must make sick?

6.
Let me be that I am and seek not to alter me.

7.
Why did you wish me milder? would you have me
False to my nature?

Rather say I play
The man I am.

8.
One may smile, and smile, and be a villain.

9.
Why, man, he doth bestride the narrow world
Like a Colossus; and we petty men
Walk under his huge legs, and peep about
To find ourselves dishonourable graves.

10.
Men in rage strike those that wish them best.

11.
So full of artless jealousy is guilt,
It spills itself in fearing to be spilt.

12.
I pray you, do not fall in love with me,
for I am falser than vows made in wine.

13.
Suspicion always haunts the guilty mind.

14.
False face must hide what the false heart doth know.

15.
Peace? I hate the word as I hate hell and all Montagues.

16.
No, no, I am but shadow of myself:
You are deceived, my substance is not here.

17.
Sir, in my heart there was a kind of fighting
That would not let me sleep.

18.
Though I am not naturally honest, I am sometimes so by chance.

19.
What a fool honesty is.

20.
Give me my robe, put on my crown;
I have Immortal longings in me.

21.
But man, proud man,
Dress'd in a little brief authority,
Most ignorant of what he's most assur'd—
His glassy essence—like an angry ape
Plays such fantastic tricks before high heaven
As makes the angels weep; who, with our spleens,
Would all themselves laugh mortal.

22.
For trust not him that hath once broken faith.

23.
Let me have war, say I: it exceeds peace as far as day does night; it's spritely, waking, audible, and full of vent. Peace is a very apoplexy, lethargy; mulled, deaf, sleepy, insensible; a getter of more bastard children than war's a destroyer of men.

24.
What a terrible era in which idiots govern the blind.

25.
These are the ushers of Martius: before him
He carries noise, and behind him he leaves tears.
Death, that dark spirit, in's nervy arm doth lie,
Which being advanc'd, declines, and then men die.

26.
O, why should wrath be mute, and fury dumb?
I am no baby, I, that with base prayers
I should repent the evils I have done:
Ten thousand worse than ever yet I did
Would I perform, if I might have my will;
If one good deed in all my life I did,
I do repent it from my very soul.

27.
Immortal gods, I crave no pelf [money];
I pray for no man but myself:
Grant I may never prove so fond,
To trust man on his oath or bond;
Or a harlot, for her weeping;
Or a dog, that seems a-sleeping:
Or a keeper with my freedom;

Or my friends, if I should need 'em.
Amen. So fall to't:
Rich men sin, and I eat root.

28.
Both my revenge and hate
loosing upon thee, in the name of justice,
Without all terms of pity.

29.
My revenges were high bent upon him
And watch'd the time to shoot.

30.
They seek revenge and therefore will not yield.

31.
She has despised me rejoicingly,
and I'll be merry in my revenge.

32.
I am very proud, revengeful,
ambitious, with more offences at my beck than
I have thoughts to put them in,
 imagination to give them shape, or time to act them in.

33.
Sin of self-love possesseth all mine eye
And all my soul and all my every part;
And for this sin there is no remedy,
it is so grounded inward in my heart

34.
Self so self-loving were iniquity.

35.
None that I love more than myself.

36.
Alack, I love myself. Wherefore? For any good
That I myself have done unto myself.

37.
[We] observed his courtship to the
common people:
How he did seem to dive into their hearts
With humble and familiar courtesy,
What reverence he did throw away on slaves.

38.
I do the wrong, and first begin to brawl.
The secret mischiefs that I set abroach.
I lay unto the grievous charge of others.

39.
What my tongue dares not that my heart shall say.

40.
Faith, there hath been many great men that have flattered the people who ne'er loved them.

41.
For conspiracy, I know not how it tastes,
though it be dished for me to try how.

42.
Think'st thou that duty shall have dread to speak
when power to flattery bows?
To plainness honor's bound when majesty falls to folly."

43.
I do nothing in the world but lie and lie in my throat.

44.
Faith, there hath been many great men
that have flattered the people
who ne'er loved them.

45.
And thus I clothe my naked villainy
With odd old ends stol'n out of holy writ;
And seem a saint, when most I play the devil.

46.
I would with such perfection
govern, sir,
T'excel the golden age.

47.
Oh, that deceit should steal such gentle shapes,
And with a virtuous vizard hide foul guile!

48.
He is my son; yea, and therein my shame;
Yet from my dugs [a woman's teat] he drew not this deceit

49.
Teach me, dear creature, how to think and speak;
Lay open to my earthy-gross conceit,
Smother'd in errors, feeble, shallow, weak,
   The folded meaning of your words' deceit.

50.
Who makes the fairest show means the most deceit.

51.
I do the wrong, and first begin to brawl.
The secret mischiefs that I set abroach
I lay unto the grievous charge of others.

I offer these following impressions as my attempt to tap into Trump's psychological state of mind, to capture as <u>literary</u>, not <u>scientific</u> necessarily, a semblance of his dark, shadow self-image (up to the gaining of the Presidency of the United States) – in the hope that they will add to the reader's understanding of Trump as an impressionistic <u>all-too-human</u> man, which he, and his followers, his devotees, falsely idealize as a <u>more-than-human</u> man.

III

CHANNELING TRUMP AS THE *ALL-TOO-HUMAN* MAN

[In Relation to His Psychological Profile]

1. *I'm here in front of you, but I'm somewhere else in back of you.*

2. *Believe me when I tell you what I don't believe.*

3. *I say what you think. Is that good or bad?*

4. *Yes, I'm honest; though I'm not sure I'm <u>morally</u> honest.*

5. *One for you, and two – if not more – for me.*

6. *Of course I love my children; but I expect them to love me more.*

7. *Don't praise me to my face; spread my word.*

8. *I can adapt myself to any situation that wins the prize I want.*

9. *Mistakes, I acknowledge; but only as a means to my successes.*

10. *Friends, I have none; acquaintances, more than I need.*

11. All that I have accumulated is actually what I have amassed for a purpose beyond possessions.

12. What have I accomplished? Everything and nothing. Everything I've aimed for, and nothing as yet I'm going to aim for.

13. I attack with a smile, with charm, with expertise, that win the day.

14. No need for me to be avaricious; wealth I've always had.

15. I know I astonish the cultured class with my boorish bombast; though much to their offended entertainment.

16. You could say that I'm autonomous – a man unto myself with underlings to clear the way.

17. How could I be wrong when I'm "on", which is almost always.

18. Racism like any other "ism" is a human bent whether overt or covert.

19. Why am I an original without a second? You may as well ask why you are not such an original.

20. My intelligence often bewilders me as I hope it does others.

21. I'm not sure about "basically", but:
Am I basically good natured, I ask myself? When I feel good, yes.
Am I basically bad-natured, I ask myself again? When I feel bad, yes.

22. Your justice may very well be my injustice.

23. I'll gaze you until you wilt, until you submit, until you break, if need be.

24. Money is everything to me so that I win everything, so that I own every-everything – so that I influence everything – all within my purview.

25. Pardon me if I "step on your toes"; you're in my way to win.
Pardon me if I stab your back; though you took the first thrust at mine.

26. Fame I need for the good (I think!) of my fellow man.

27. For war I'd risk peace; for peace, I'd risk war.

28. You need to be loved; I need to be needed, not foremost by others, but for my calling.

29. Serve me and I'll serve you – though most likely not in your best interests depending upon the extent of your loyalty.

30. Knowing that I'm wondrous to myself, how can I accept my poor mortality! – here I am; there I was. Sad.

31. Am I generous person? Yes, for utility's sake.

32. Am I courageous person? To win, to please, the plaudits of my fellow man, I would run into a burning building to save a life.

33. Am I good person? To myself, of course, then for you if you deserve it.

34. Am I a man of integrity? Don't expect it on your terms.

35. Yes, I have a warm, smiling personality to please; but I warn you, don't get too close to the real me. Who is the real me? Better you should ask: <u>What</u> is the real me?

36. When most do I fail myself? When others fail me.

37. When am I most vulnerable? When I'm asleep.

38. Who comes first my family or me? My family, of course. Who comes first my family or my work? My family of course. Who comes first my family or my mission? My mission, of course?

39. Am I as mean-spirited, as it may appear? Basically or conditionally? Well, basically I am a hollow man receptive strongly to everything human – that is: all-too-human.

40. Am I capable of all-encompassing, intense, endearing, passionate love? That's a tall order, for sure. Well, I would never have been so immensely and worldly successful if I weren't so loving, in my way.

41. Am I basically of a hard or soft nature? How could I be so ruthlessly ambitious, commanding, demanding, controlling, were I basically soft-nature. Silly question.

42. I am foremost creative not destructive – but creative destructively, if you know what I mean.

43. I'll lie for my truth whether true or not.

44. Am I dangerous? Be sure of it if you get in my way; and often enough when I get in your way.

45. For me, in sum, my self-interest exceeds and rules your self-interest.

46. How do I recognize jealousy (harm) against me? It's all in the eyes, in the expression, in the response; which requires a fine-tuning perception to detect it.

47. All that glitters is gold in my material, sensuous world.

48. I'm hated by some so much that they love me – not as a person, mind you, but as an icon. Why would I want to be loved otherwise? Much of what I say might be illogical; yet it is my illogic by which logic asserts itself. So in a sort of inverted way, I'm really a very logical guy.

49. No, I'm not an intellectual sort of thinker; rather, I think intuitively; which, if I'm not mistaken, precedes intelligence.

50. You say I'm a ruthless opportunist, out to get what you I want no matter the means. Would not that make me evil? Yet Malcolm X, out for justice and freedom, declares "by whatever means necessary." Would he then not be considered a ruthless opportunist for his agenda? Is he then evil as well? Different ends, but the same means.

51. I'm a primitive, to be sure: I survive by tooth and claw; by an eye for an eye. Yet I add to these two truths (some consider them half-truths – fools!): coccyx, a lie for a lie.

52. No one would ever mistake what I deem as showy, as tawdry; perhaps in some cases gaudy.

53. Subclass of women: tarts – my kind of women on my evenings out with the "boys". Out for a good time and that is all; then home I go.

54. I don't consider myself invulnerable to the deceptions of others; after all, I can't know everything. Yet even my losses, are wins, since I always get even in one way or another, at one time or another.

55. Women! If you're frigid for whatever reason, come see about me.

56. When it comes to the more women ("loose" women, that is) the better (or worse in some cases); then that is what would be expected, or understood, of a man in my supreme position. You know, the female draw to the alpha dog – survival of the fittest instinct, so it's written.

57. Alright, I admit it, beautiful women are my addiction; but then so is my work. The former is a relief; the latter, <u>the</u> relief.

58. Have I been promiscuous? Always. How could I help it being who I am when women are always at my front door, so to speak.

59. Whatever love I might feel toward women in general, other than the motherly, friendly type, is foremost aphrodisiac.

60. I oftentimes seduce with my smile and childlike "naïveté". Can you believe it, some women want to mother me! – after you know what, that is to say.

61. I've been legally interrogated so many times over the years; and here I am a noncriminal and a billionaire.

62. Fun for me is work for others.

63. Foreign countries with whom I've always gotten along well; for basically, we are all economists of the highest order.

64. I was handsome and charismatic in my golden youth; and now in the "yellow leaf" of age, I am Moses sculpted in marble awed to be seen [RE: Michelangelo's statue, Moses].

65. You might wonder, am I an advocate of justice and wisdom or of injustice and ignorance? As I see it, I support justice for the just, wisdom for the wise, injustice for the unjust, and ignorance for the ignorant. This answer I think is what is called begging the question or circular reasoning – one of those or both or the same. I'm good at this kind of reasoning, as you can tell.

66. I've said, "have the courage to be who you are." Now that's worthy advice for latent heroes, but worthless advice for latent cowards.

67. I'm not guilty of avarice, since I don't hoard my wealth; I risk it.

68. Do I suffer much? Only when I fail to get what I want or need; which is not "much" I grant.

69. Sensitivity is not one of my virtues. What, would you have me victimized by the soft-hearted, or hard-hearted ones?

70. Stress I can deal with since I've inoculated myself against it. Yet I need periodic injections. From what source? Diet coke! – just kidding; an inside joke!

71. As you know, I like the fight to prove again and again the truth of the old adage that might is right. Even it's wrong at times, I'll fight knowing that I'll lose. It keeps me agitated.

72. I don't do my dirty work. I have thugs do that for me; I call them my bodyguards.

73. "Love Me or Leave Me" – My favorite song title says it spot-on for me, all around, regarding human relationships.

74. I frown on the flimflam man who sneaks his money from others for his pockets only.

75. Keat's "Truth is beauty; beauty truth" in my version goes like this: My truth is beauty; my beauty truth."

76. I'm a showman par excellence to show myself in splendor and sell my wares for all to see – and pay.

77. Though I smile and "joke around", I'm dead serious when it comes to business before – and instead of – pleasure.

78. I want – actually, need – not only admiration (what a bore!) but out-and-out adoration; not on your knees, nor in your heart, but in your mind: all for me.

79. I'll promise anything you want to hear, so long as you expect it of me however long it takes, whatever might interfere –<u>Do you know what I mean</u>?

80. You can bet that I'm sure of myself even more than 100 percent; but you will lose that bet when all bets are over; which, with me, you never know when (I'm not sure of myself).

81. My agenda of all that I do and think is self-promotion; no doubt about it. How could all my wondrous deeds have been accomplished otherwise?

82. My detractors say of me how much they hate me; and most likely they do; yet they follow my every move (which I furnish them in all the media), enchanted by my uniqueness. Is this not a hate that loves?

83. Yes, I am Narcissus adoring, fixated by, my reflection by a pool (mirror). When will I learn that such love cannot be reciprocated?

84. Acquisitive for possessions, I am not; but for the thrill and the deal, and the honor, I am.

85. I don't <u>have</u> friends; I win them,

86. Reading keeps me informed, not enlightened.

87. Passion? I'm always on about passion; without which there's no fire in the blood, only embers; and for a person of fiery passion like myself, that fire is a firestorm.

88. How is it possible for me to be humble when I'm so mountainous.

89. Altruism, I don't believe in simply because I have the means; though I give as I must. It's either that or be taxed. At least with altruism, my name is stamped favorably for it; whereas with taxes, my name is recorded legally – at least as best and safest I know of.

90. Life is fillet mignon and lobster for the likes of my kind.

91. Yes, I said that you have to treat women like s--t; but that was said in the context of: if they themselves are of the same worth.

92. The touchy question is: Do I admire evil dictators, whoever they may be? Certainly not their person, and certainly not their horrors; but as captains of "Satan" (that is, human Evil) they're as admirable as captains of God as to their attainments. Yet, keep in mind that these evil ones are as much "crucified" for their ways no less than the good ones.

93. When I'm told that I contradict myself, I always reply with our American poet, Walt Whitman, "Do I contradict myself? Very well, then I contradict myself, I am large, I contain multitudes."

94. I advocate wealth for the wealthy, elitism for the elite, power for the powerful; but never greed for the greedy.

95. I am an American aristocrat, of the "House of Lords" luxuriating in my titleship, to pass on to my progeny; not realizing, nor wanting to realize, the historical finality of such glorification.

96. I certainly can be affable when need be, even when want be.

97. I'd like to make an announcement about myself that I rarely admit: I really am antisocial in a way inasmuch as I don't like small talk, nor camaraderie; however sociable or charming I may appear in public. Granted I need the social scene to feel myself alive and important and needed and honored and adored; who wants to see and hear others' concerns or interests or babbling. Leave me alone. What I have to put up with to get what I want. It's a cross that I bear.

98. Any anxiety I might feel stems from losing my composure, my authority. You know the truth that smarts us like a dart in the thigh: "If I'm wrong in one regard, they'll think me wrong in all regards."

99. Toward those I've harmed unfairly, it's hard for me to feel remorse since it was a fight to the finish and I had to kick them while they were down, so to speak. I just don't think of it. While in the fray, I get enraged and "lose it" and

play dirty. I'm a fighter after all; and not a fair one when my dignity is smarted, or assets are threatened. And on top of it, I don't take losing easily; I will not slink away.

100. By "bad" you can include bad-tempered and bad-mannered, at times; but "bad-willed" almost always. What remains of me is good-will toward others sometimes.

101. What I do may at times be ugly; but oh, what beautiful edifices emerge from such ugliness.

102. Bankruptcy, little known, is part of my game. Why do you think I call myself the "king of debt" with such pride. And my game? To win and to lose; to lose then to win. I play both sides of the game like a "card shark" shuffling the cards seemingly in my favor.

103. Am I not as civilized and cultured as befits my image? Who could doubt it. How then could you "see" the barbarian in me? By my actions if you look closely enough, and by my glare if you shudder at it.

104. I know when to bludgeon my opponent and when to embrace him.

105. Braggadocio will get you everywhere – if you're rich and powerful and mighty, that is; like me.

106. I'm thought of as broad-minded because I speak my mind; however, what I speak of knows nothing, or little, of wisdom proper: that is, of spiritual and transcendent matters. I go by the maxim: "Knowledge is power" and the morality of relativism.

107. I'll camouflage myself into every enterprise worthy of my time and effort.

108. My campaign in the ultimate? To rule my history.

109. "Love is all you need'" Right you are Lennon. I believe it emphatically. I love myself, I love my work, I love my mission, I love my family, I love my properties, I love vanilla ice cream, I love war, I love peace . . . I could go on and on without stop.

110. I'll listen to your take on this matter, let it pass by me, possibly with this or that tidbit of an idea from you, then do what I was going to do anyway.

111. Okay, I am the wizard of lies, such that who would have seen it coming? Who would have thought it? Who would have believed it? Now that's wizardry. You catch them in bewilderment. Then you make sure they cannot think straight. Then you have them in your "rabbit's hat".

112. My carnality keeps me all-too-human when I would be more-than-human. Both can be a bother to me at times; otherwise, I'm fine with being a man in the middle: not quite sure of what or who I am.

113. I keep myself familiar with the criminal element about me; it's here to stay, and so am I. Not to say that I'm guilty of any criminal act, but that I've used some of their strategies within the law if not within ethical or just principles. Life is a duality, is it not.

114. When I win I feel myself master of life –Watch out You! When I lose, I feel a slave to life – Watch out me!

115. For me, excess is a virtue, not a vice, as old Aristotle would argue contrarily.

116. How is it possible for me to be humble when I'm so mountainous.

117. Secretly, I'm afflicted with limitations – though, just as secretly, I know there are no secrets.

118. I can be affectionate . . . when the feeling surprises me.

119. I'm an allurement to the wrong people who flock to me.

120. I'm aloof to the affairs of the heart; its heat stifles me.

121. Yes, I boast and brag, and love myself "to death". How else can I face and bear my insecurities, my anxieties.

122. I am benumbed of sentiment, though certainly not of emotion – raw emotion at my worst.

123. I bestride "lady luck", rough for the ride.

124. I've been blessed with the eye of the tiger ready always to pounce.

125. Will I break down mentally if I keep on like this? Very likely. Opposition is all too relentless, as age wearies us; what was once welcome stays too long.

126. A magnificent showman I am on board a fanciful showboat steaming along the Mississippi, parading my gifts for all to see.

127. I'm a capitalist par excellence, as everyone who knows, or knows about me; though without in the least being interested in large scale financial matters. Capitalism just happens to be my "ism" in which I'm able to make more money than anyone else in my field, for more vistas than in my field. If I could do so under communism or socialism or egalitarianism, I would be a socialist, or communist, or egalitarianist, and whatever else. But here I am a Republican.

128. So many caricatures of me! Keep them coming. They all add to my mystique, keep me highlighted, for a laugh or a derision.

129. I keep myself familiar with the criminal element about me; it's here to stay, and so am I. Not to say that I'm guilty of any criminal act, but that I've

used some of their strategies within the law if not within ethical nor just principles. Life is a duality.

130. They say I commit one logical fallacy after another. Whenever did I embrace reason when my "Reason" supersedes logical reason.

131. Neither happiness nor joy caress my mighty life, only doses of daily pleasures.

132. I've read it stated that I'm a victim of arrested development, that psychologically I'm more adolescent than mature. What do I have to reply to such an absurd accusation? "Absurd" that's what! Though I do admit to some adolescent fixed traits trailing my thoughts and behavior. They're kind of embarrassing to me; but what can I do about them; they're part of my mind set.

And aren't we not all subject to this psychological pattern, more or less? But, "arrested development"? Me? Please, don't insult my intelligence nor my accomplishments, nor my family unity. Grow up!

SECTION II
Trump as Overman?

PART FOUR

Revealed by Others and this Author

[A new type of thinking is essential if mankind is to survive and move towards higher levels. No problem can be solved from the same level of consciousness that creates it.]
- Einstein (physicist)

The Overman and Trump

Part Four explores the possibility that Trump may be related to the **overman** concept (translated in German, übermensch) meaning the ideal superior man/woman of the future, introduced by the 19th century philosopher-psychologist-prophet, Friedrich Nietzsche.

PRELUDE:
The Trump/ Nietzsche Overman Question
in Tandem with Trump's Rise to the American Presidency

i

The underlying theme to this study of Donald Trump is that his unparalleled life, character, and accomplishments, define him as a man of destiny, an unexpected historic necessity, meant to broaden the future of entrepreneurial, social, and political landscape from the past and of our times.

Having to be embroiled in these three fields, required, first of all, that he play the 'role' as part of them; while all the time, as a wolf in sheep's disguise, he acted as an orca amidst sharks in order for him to surpass their traditional stolid, mired, beliefs and values.

Having reached the ostentatious pinnacle of his real estate profession, he next made his mark in the entertainment field (beauty pageant, TV show, sports), and thereby became an American iconic celebrity.

During these two phases of utmost accomplishments, he had "dabbled" in political matters on the side – preparing for his next foray into the realm of politics: the American Presidency, no less. And just as his accomplishments peaked in his former conquests, he went on to conquer the political gambit by winning the election as the President of the United States in 2016: leader of the free world, master of world events.

ii

I suggest that we continue to observe this titan, this colossus, as a man of destiny of the highest order, not as a *physical* warlord like any of the historic figures who have played their role by physical conquest costing the upheaval and horror of innumerable lives and events while partitioning nations into political landscapes. That form of thousands of years of conquest has been long over – we can say it had its historic purpose (though few nations are still arguing down that prospect). What has been formulating since that historical finality, has, in our times, transmuted into what can be termed *psychological* conquest. Conquest not by wars of bloodshed, massacre, torture, slavery, and land-plunder, but by wars of *mind control*. The warlord, Mr. Trump portrays has all the earmarks of this *psychological* conquest in which men/women worldwide will be subservient to the Man/Woman manipulative control through international inflexible laws, intoxicants/drugs, subterfuge, 'conspicuous consumption', endless comforts, public surveillance, religious subversion (all shades of *Brave New World*, especially) – the rule, not by physical force but by *force of will*; that is to say, basically by injustice and ignorance. What we realistic-idealists propose is just the opposite ideology: rule by force of *character*, by means of justice and wisdom.

iii

My main concerns are: how did this exceptional man – obviously a genius of affairs ... and a scoundrel of sorts – do it? Did he "know" right from his childhood that he would one day become the President of the United States, and more? And having the right temperament, the right intuitive intellect, the right will, the right personality, the right circumstances, the right parents, the right wealth, he reached his ultimate goal, step by step, stage by stage, though it took him almost fifty years. That attainment certainly proves to be a long, ranged ambition, aspiration, to bear for an ordinary man even with his extraordinary gifts.

iv

Yet, he never considered himself an ordinary mortal by any measurement, nor even an extraordinary man – that was always understood; rather his stance was that of a supreme man, a superman. By a 'superman', he would mean a man of super powers that transcended mere human powers; someone like a Napoleon, Caesar, Alexander, who somehow or other was in touch with the universal Mind, or Power. Could it be he considers himself a demigod: a god-idol amongst men?

It is in this frame of reference that I consider Trump as a man of destiny; certainly not his humanistic accomplishments, but regarding the advancement, the ascendancy of our human species through his *underlying*, most likely, *unwittingly*, trans-human, evolutionary, transformative accomplishments. Yet, this marvel of a scenario attributed to Trump is all for the purpose of awakening the people from their slumber so that they may move forward with their true collective purpose. Mr. Trump acts as the dangerous rickety bridge that must be crossed in order to get to the other side where an advancing culture resides. This 'act' heralds him, unquestionably, as mentioned (and will continue to mention in order to impress awaringly in the reader's mind), an 'historic necessity'.

But is this "historic necessity" in any way related to the overman concept?

In answer, let us observe what Nietzsche himself has to say regarding his extraordinary overman concept.

NIETZSCHE ON THE OVERMAN

1

[Selections mostly from Nietzsche's Thus Spoke Zarathustra, The Will to Power, Beyond Good and Evil ...]

INTRODUCTORY NOTE

My purpose in the following extended quotations by Nietzsche himself is to defend his paradigm of the overman concept against superficial, incomplete, misleading, interpretations; and by doing so, to place his main underlying purpose and meaning of it in its proper understanding. From this point, we can approach Trump's association, or disassociation, with Nietzsche's overman concept.

"The overman (übermensch) concept, for Nietzsche, aims essentially toward the further evolution of humankind through the transformation of man's all-too-human side made *more-than-human*. Nietzsche sees humanity as facing an unprecedented crisis in [his time and] our times which will require a transformation of values and beliefs, ideas and ideals, for evolution of humankind. The following passage continues his overman concept in his *Beyond Good and Evil*:

"With the strength of his – [man's new-found nobility (overman's stance)] – spiritual eye and insight grows distance and, as it were, the space around man: his world becomes more profound; ever new stars, ever new riddles and images become visible for him. Perhaps everything on which the spirit's eye has exercised its acuteness and thoughtfulness was nothing but an occasion for this exercise, a playful matter, something for children and those who are childish. Perhaps the day will come when the most solemn concepts which have caused the most fights and suffering, the concepts "God" and "sin," will seem no more important to us than child's toy and a child's pain seem to an old man—and perhaps "the old man" will then be in need of another toy and another pain – still child enough, an eternal!"

1. Dead are all gods: now we want the overman to live.

2. Man is something that shall be overcome. Man is a rope, tied between beast and overman – a rope over an abyss. What is great in man is that he is a bridge and not an end.

3. Not "mankind" but "overman" is the goal.

4. What I can love in man is this, that he is a transition and a decline.

5. It lies within our nature to create a being higher than ourselves.

6. In spite of all, he must come to us, this *redeeming* man ... who gives the earth its purpose ... this victory over God and nothingness.

7. Behold, I bring you the Overman! The Overman is the meaning of the earth. Let your will say: The Overman shall be the meaning of the earth! I beg of you

my brothers, remain true to the earth, and believe not those who speak to you of otherworldly hopes! Poisoners are they, whether they know it or not. Despisers of life are they, decaying ones and poisoned ones themselves, of whom the earth is weary: so away with them!

8. Remain faithful to the earth, my brothers, with the power of your virtue. Let your gift-giving love and your knowledge serve the meaning of the earth. Thus, I beg and beseech you. Do not let them flyaway from earthly things and beat with their wings against eternal walls. Alas, there has always been so much virtue that has flown away. Lead back to the earth the virtue that flew away, as I do – back to the body, back to life, that it may give the earth a meaning, a human meaning.

9. Some time, in a stronger age than this mouldy, self-doubting present, he will come to us, the redeeming man of great love and contempt ... This man of the future will redeem us not just from the ideal held up till now, but also from the things which have to arise from it, from the great nausea, the will to nothingness, from nihilism, that stroke of midday and of the great decision which makes the will free again, which gives earth its purpose and man his hope again, this antichrist and anti-nihilist, this conqueror of God and nothingness – he must come one day.

10. I love those who do not first seek a reason beyond the stars for *going down* and being sacrifices, but sacrifice themselves to the earth, that the earth of the overman may hereafter arrive.

11. I love him who lives in order to know, and seeks to know in order that the overman may hereafter live.

12. I will teach men the meaning of their existence: the Overman, the lightning out of the dark cloud- man.

13. What is great in man is that he is a bridge and not a goal: what is lovable in man is that he is an OVER-GOING [self-transcending to the ever-broadening discoveries of human consciousness] and a DOWN-GOING [Untergang] ([self-exploring into the darkened depths of discovery].

14. In truth, man is a polluted river. One must be a sea to receive a polluted river without becoming defiled. I bring you the Overman! He is that sea; in him your great contempt can be submerged.

15. You shall love beyond yourselves some day! So first, learn to love. And for that you have to drink the bitter cup of your love.

16. All beings so far have created something beyond themselves; and do you want to be the ebb of this great flood and even go back to the beasts rather than overcome man? What is the ape to man? A laughingstock or a painful

embarrassment. And man shall be just that for the overman: a laughingstock or a painful embarrassment ...

17. *Originality*. – What is originality? To see something that still has no name; that still cannot be named even though it is lying right before everyone's eyes. The way people usually are, it takes a name to make something visible at all. – Those with originality have usually been the name-givers.

18. What makes one heroic [as overman]? – To approach at the same time one's highest suffering and one's highest hope.

19. What do you believe in? – In this: that the weight of all things must be determined anew.

20. What does your conscience say? – 'You should become who you are. '

21. Where lie your greatest dangers? – In compassion.

22. What do you love in others? – My hopes.

23. Whom do you call bad? – He who always wants to put people to shame.

24. What is most human to you? – To spare someone shame.

25. What is the seal of having become free? – No longer to be ashamed before oneself.

26. Every kind of contempt for sex, every impurification of it by means of the concept "impure", is the crime par excellence against life – is the real sin against the holy spirit of life.

[Compare: *"The generative forces* of the world are wholesome, and there is no destructive poison in them". (*Wisdom of Solomon, Old Testament*)]

27. The need to show that as the consumption of man and mankind becomes more and more economical and the "machinery" of interests and services in integrated even more intricately, a counter-movement is inevitable. I designate this as the secretion of a luxury surplus of mankind: it aims to bring to light a stronger species, a higher type that arises and preserves itself under different conditions from those of the average man. My concept, my metaphor, for this type is, as one knows, the word "overman."

28. The search for truth is still the greatest (and only sensible) form of rebellion.

29. What is important is the might of the soul that decrees death to death and dedicates itself to eternal life.

30. What matters what becomes of us if a minute of such detachment gives us at last the purity of vision in which things are seen apart from the light, in

which they are colored by our sorrow, our disillusionment, our lassitude, our greed or our enthusiasm?

31. Paraphrasing Saint Paul, I say, "I, yet not I, but Spinoza's God, dwelleth in me," the God who sees all tragedies through the eyes of eternity where the anger and the evil of the moment become the love and the good of the ages. ... *Let us stamp the impress of eternity upon our lives!* [my italics] Let us live that we may desire to live again: this is my creed, yesterday, today, tomorrow, and the yesterdays to follow tomorrow.

32. I once described the evil principle in Nature as our eternal inability to find what we seek. But when did Nature ever agree to make us a partner to her secrets? And how much more dreadful things might be if we found half the things we look for!

Having thuswise made it clear in Nietzsche's own words what he means by the Overman; and that this meaning is essentially a new *humanistic spirituality*, or otherwise stated, a *transcendent morality*, within and beyond good and evil, let us now derive an overview of selected, historical, noted, personages whose lives and works accord, more or less, with Nietzsche's overman ideal to-come.

2
The Following Selected Exemplars
Related to, are, and would-be supporters of the Overman Concept

SRI AUROBINDO

Sri Aurobindo (Bengali; born Aurobindo Ghose; 15 August 1872 – 5 December 1950) was an Indian nationalist, philosopher, yogi, guru and poet.

"The step from man to superman [overman] is the next approaching achievement in the earth's evolution. There lies our destiny and the liberating key to our aspiring, but troubled and limited human existence – inevitable because it is at once the intention of the inner Spirit and the logic of Nature's process."

MOHANDAS GANDHI

Mohandas Karamchand Gandhi 2 October 1869 – 30 January 1948) was the leader of the Indian independence movement against British rule.

"If India adopted the doctrine of love as an active part of her religion and introduced it in her politics, Swaraj (Home rule or Self-Rule) would descend upon India from heaven."

PIERRE TEILHARD DE CHARDIN

Pierre Teilhard de Chardin (French) (1 May 1881 – 10 April 1955) was a French idealist philosopher and Jesuit priest.

"There is almost a sensual longing for communion with others who have a large vision. The immense fulfillment of the friendship between those engaged in furthering the evolution of consciousness has a quality impossible to describe. ... Love is a sacred reserve of energy; it is like the blood of spiritual evolution."

ABRAHAM MASLOW

Abraham Harold Maslow (April 1, 1908 – June 8, 1970) was an American psychologist who was best known for creating Maslow's hierarchy of needs.

"We fear our highest possibilities. We are generally afraid to become that which we can glimpse in our most perfect moments, under conditions of great courage. We enjoy and even thrill to godlike possibilities we see in ourselves in such peak moments. And yet we simultaneously shiver with weakness, awe, and fear before these very same possibilities."

MARTIN LUTHER KING JR.

Martin Luther King Jr. (born Michael King Jr., January 15, 1929 – April 4, 1968) was an American Baptist minister and activist who became the most visible spokesperson and leader in the Civil Rights Movement.

"I have a dream that my four little children will one day live in a nation where they will not be judged by the color of their skin but by the content of their character."

MUHAMMAD

Muhammad (Arabic: c. 570 CE – 8 June 632 CE) is the prophet and founder of Islam.

"You will never enter heaven until you have faith; and you will not complete your faith until you love one another."

ABRAHAM LINCOLN

Abraham Lincoln was the 16th President of the United States, serving from March 1861 until his assassination in April 1865.

"I happened to be placed, being a humble instrument in the hands of our Heavenly Father, as I am, and as we all are, to work out His great purposes, I have desired that all my works and acts may be according to His will, and that it might be so, I have sought His aid; but if, after endeavoring to do my best in the light which He affords me, I find my efforts fail, I must believe that for some purpose unknown to me, He wills it otherwise."

CONFUCIUS

Confucius, 551– 479 BCE, was a Chinese teacher, editor, politician, and philosopher

"The way of the superior person is threefold: virtuous, they are free from anxieties; wise they are free from perplexities; and bold they are free from fear."

JESUS CHRIST

Jesus c. 4 BC – c. 30/33 AD), also referred to as Jesus of Nazareth or Jesus Christ, was a Jewish preacher and religious leader who became the central figure of Christianity.

"Behold! The Kingdom of God is within you."

JOHN LENNON

John Lennon, MBE (born John Winston Lennon; 9 October 1940 – 8 December 1980) was an English guitarist, singer, and songwriter who founded the Beatles, the most commercially successful and musically influential band in the history of popular music.

You say you'll change the constitution
Well, you know
We all want to change your head
You tell me it's the institution
Well, you know
You better free you mind instead

3

TRUMP'S SEEMING RELATIONSHIP TO THE OVERMAN

This glowing image of President-elect Donald Trump, enshrouded in a white mist, glorifies his victorious entrance as demigod to his adoring multitudes. [YouTube]

It was this image above that most likely sparked my thought that possibly Trump considered himself Nietzsche's *übermensch* (i.e. overman). Accordingly, I researched this possibility and all that follows on this matter.

THE TRUMP OVERMAN INTERNET ARTICLES

The articles taken from the internet indicate that others have surmised the possible connection, between Donald Trump and Nietzsche's übermensch; translated as overman (or otherwise named "superman").

The following two articles, especially, I quote in full for the reason that, one, bears on Mr. Persico's contention that Trump is surely an overman in a more or less positive sense ["postmodern god"] of Nietzsche's conception of it; and the other, Mr. Coleman Luck's contention the Trump is as well Nietzsche's overman; yet in a negative sense ["the American over man"] of Nietzsche's conception of the overman by comparing him with world leaders of the type as Napoleon and Hitler, and the like; and being an overthrower of conventional morality for the sake of self-enhancement. The remaining articles, of which I

give the titles are evidently opposed to Trump as overman; yet, I believe that the authors do not have an understanding grasp of Nietzsche's conception of the overman.

(i) Donald Trump as a Postmodern God | Dr.Tomer Persico | 10/03/2016

The phenomenon of Donald Trump, his meteoric rise in the Republican halls of fame, has many reasons. Rage against the establishment, White Man's fears, lower class economic distress and more. But I believe we cannot fully understand the massive support for the man if we fail to notice one major dimension thereof, which constitutes the source of his unique charisma.

Let me put it this way: Trump is a postmodern god.

Of course, he is very rich and can therefore do as he wishes and supposedly doesn't need to take anyone else's wishes and opinions into consideration. That's true, but the issue runs deeper. As a god, Trump must be not only omnipotent, but also distant and invulnerable. As a postmodern god, that distance and immunity must come against a backdrop of his breaking the rules, his being an *übermensch* [overman] who undermines conventions. And just as important, from within that distance, the postmodern god must convey emotion, warmth.

To be sure, Trump excels at undermining conventions. He says whatever he likes, be it defamatory, racist, ridicule or dirty words that no candidate has ever dared use. Equally important, he is defiantly not conforming to the conventions of standard Republican conservatism. The fact that he is not a classic conservative (used to be a Democrat, was pro-choice, pro-government intervention in property and so on) helps him in that regard because it magnifies his otherness, and thus the perception that he's not one of us. He's superior.

But all this would not have been enough had it not been for Trump's ability to project authenticity. This is achieved in a postmodern society by full equation between inside and outside, by breaking down the barrier between the subjective and the objective. Trump, as is well known, says anything that comes to his head at any given moment. He hides nothing. What you see is what you get. Not only that, but he is shameless. He has no internal space separate from the external, that could supposedly have reservations about whatever is going on outside.

Trump is a moving display of spontaneity and directness, with no judgment, planning or hesitation. Therefore, he cannot be considered "fake" or "phony" (the cardinal sins of our time). His heart is open, and even if it is ugly, it's not its content but the gesture of revealing it that matters to his admirers. Even if he says harsh things, to their mind he hides nothing from them, he is authentic, and that is the matter.

And yet, Trump doesn't blow his top, doesn't lose control, doesn't fume, doesn't cry, and doesn't scream. He's cool. In other words, he's immune. He's warm, and yet distant. He speaks from the heart and to the heart, and yet is invulnerable. American sociologist Richard Sennett noticed back in the 1970's that this is how public attraction to a leader is built nowadays. "Controlled spontaneity," he claimed, arouses sympathy and admiration in us, and the feeling that the person in front of us can be believed. This is what postmodern charisma means.

People believe in a pre-modern god. They have faith in a postmodern god. This trust is bestowed not because the things the god says are logical and not because his political plans are sound. Their trust is given because he, as said above, projects reliability, that is to say, authenticity. In this regard Trump brings our tendency to prefer form to content to a peak: his credibility stems from the way he expresses himself, not from what his expressions mean.

It's fun to watch a post-modern god. His audience doesn't want to be his friend – obviously such a man has no real friends – his audience wants to be his audience. Since the show must go on, the audience will vote for him. The way to stop him is not to tell his audience that he is evil ("Hitler"), that is by turning him into a devil (for there is no difference in form between a devil and a god). The way to stop him is by turning him into a man. This can be accomplished by making him lose his composure, by humiliating him.

(ii) **Over Man: The Temptation of Donald Trump** *Coleman Luck* July 26, 2016

I missed it. Over all the months, as I have been trying to argue people away from voting for Mr. Trump, I failed to understand what was really going on. But since his speech at the convention, everything has become very, very clear. I now believe that his election is inevitable. Both as a candidate and a man, he is a force that we have never encountered in American Presidential politics. He calls his following a "movement" and he is correct. Progressives desperately struggle to place him into a category that they can understand and which will allow them to diminish his impact. In their blind idealism, they cannot imagine that such a man could be elected. Over and over they mumble that "America is better than that." No, America is not better than that and there are reasons why.

But conservatives make their own terrible mistake from the other side. They hear only what Mr. Trump wants them to hear and call him one of their own. In their naïve desperation, they think that he views promises and agreements in the same way they do. He doesn't. It is very clear for anyone not locked into an iron-clad political viewpoint that Donald Trump is neither a conservative nor a progressive. So what is he?

At the end of the 19th century, German philosopher, Friedrich Nietzsche wrote a book entitled Thus Spake Zarathustra. It was a compilation of his many thoughts, dreams, disappointments and sorrows. The book is not easy to understand, but one thing is clear in this and all of his writings. Beyond all else, Nietzsche hated Christianity and the Christian God. He considered this religion an ultimate statement of weakness that presented a pusillanimous deity, so powerless that all he could do was die on a cross. Far worse, this horrible weakness had spread like a hellish disease totally destroying the strength and grandeur of the ancient Greco/Roman world. Nietzsche's desperate hope and dream was to see that evil influence eradicated. He pronounced the "death of God", by which he meant that since the Christian God was now dead, destroyed by 18th and 19th century Rationalism, the morality of the Bible was dead as well. What was left? Nothing. The only truth was that there was no truth, and, for Nietzsche, this opened great possibilities. In his view, belief in the Christian God was the monstrous impede ment restraining humanity from reaching its proper evolutionary destination. In *Thus Spake Zarathustra* he called for a new breed of human set free from the theological and moral chains of the past.

What would this new human look like?

He would be an individual filled with such a dynamic life force that he would "create" his own existence. And he would do so without relying on metaphysical concepts such as God or the soul. Nietzsche called this new man "übermensch", which translates into English as "Over Man" or "Super Man". I won't use that second translation because it conjures up a trite comic book character. Physical strength is not the issue. This Super Man personifies a kind of transcendent energy that empowers everything he does.

According to Nietzsche, the übermensch is above the rest of humanity, enslaved as we are to the herd instinct. He is deeply aware that the rules of common morality do not apply to him. He makes his own rules and answers only to himself. He understands that power exists for its own sake and only a man who is self-possessed has the right to grasp and wield it. By his actions, the übermensch deeply influences enslaved humanity toward a new, liberated world. Among philosophers, there is heated disagreement about the application of Nietzsche's philosophy, but regarding one fact they all agree. What he wrote has had a deep influence on all of us.

We have seen them before.

According to Nietzsche the Over Man could appear and exert powerful influence in many areas of human society. He could be a great author or composer. But what would he be like if he rose to prominence in politics and government? Nietzsche viewed Napoleon as an excellent example of an übermensch in national leadership. Though he was dead before they appeared, both Benito Mussolini and Adolph Hitler were influenced by his writings and certainly both considered themselves examples Over Men as did their millions of followers. Nietzsche's sister, who became the custodian of his work, passionately believed that Hitler fit her brother's description. Both the German Nazis and the Italian Fascists considered Nietzsche to be a seminal influence on their beliefs. Based on the history of these national leaders, is it possible to see a pattern in the way an Over Man can take power?

First, the national environment must be right. The Man must meet The Moment. In France, Germany and Italy, the Over Man stepped onto the national stage at a time of deep crisis. In each country there was economic turmoil and great division that included violence. Feeling powerless in their suffering, citizens were filled with rage and desperation. More importantly, in each of these countries there had been a terrible loss of national identity. Millions of deeply patriotic citizens were utterly disillusioned with establishment leaders and desperate for a man who was strong enough to make things right and give them back their national soul.

Second, these "Over Men" were not given the right to lead a country with dictatorial powers based on their experience and qualifications. They were not given the right simply because they told the people what they wanted to hear. Certainly, each one spoke to his nation about their suffering, danger, economic crises and common enemies, but the appeal was on an entirely different level. How did they give hope and a vision for the future? Each of these Over Men told his nation not simply that he *had* the answers to all their problems.

He told them that he *was* the answer.

What amazing arrogance! Why did millions believe and blindly follow, entrusting these dangerous men with their nations and their lives? Like sheep staring into the eyes of a wolf, they fell under the power of an overwhelming personality. This Power has nothing to do with physical attractiveness or even personal charm. It is a dynamic, predatory magnetism that draws people to itself. The choice to believe and follow is never a rational one. It is purely emotional supported by the shallowest of justifications. Historically, this is how wolves take control.

Third, once people had vested their faith in these Over Men, they followed and defended them all the way to national destruction as if these leaders were their own flesh and blood. Once in power, every promise that an Over Man kept was applauded and every promise not kept was blamed on others. The Over Men clearly understood the terrifying freedom that this gave them and used it. As Donald Trump has said, he could go out and shoot someone and it wouldn't matter. He is right. His followers would find reasons to believe that the action was justified. By placing their faith in an Over Man, it is as though they attach themselves spiritually and psychologically to him. How far can this go? The dictators in question did great evil, but their followers overlooked and excused it as though they were blind. Why? Because individual citizens had so identified with the Übermensch that to convict him of wrong was the same as convicting themselves. They loved him like they loved themselves. And so they became complicit in all the evil things that were done. The first step of believing in and supporting such men led inexorably to all the others.

Fourth, the more intelligent and sophisticated the citizen, the deeper he or she fell under the power of the Over Man. In the 1930's Germany was arguably the most sophisticated and educated country in the world. From the highest to the lowest, the people fell under the power of Hitler's personality. Some of his most passionate followers were in the university and in the church. The same kind of fall took place in France and Italy.

Did these leaders deliver on their deepest promises?

For periods of time, each one did. France, Germany and Italy did become great again. Each country rose from degradation to prominence and power on the world stage. Internally, some economic wrongs were righted.

Governmental systems were made to work better. Most importantly, new, potent, national identities were sculpted. How was this done? It was accomplished because these nations gave themselves up to be reshaped in the image of the Over Man. In the process each dictator came to personify the nation he dominated. Napoleon didn't just rule France, he *was* France. Hitler didn't just rule Germany, he *was* Germany. And the same was true for Mussolini in Italy. This perception was not simply the fantasy of a single, arrogant mind. It was a fervent, religious belief in the hearts of their countrymen. Due to the overwhelming power of their personalities, these men became the fathers of their nations. Parents named their children after them and requested that they be the godfathers. Mussolini received 1500 letters a day from passionate admirers.

How does all of this relate to the United States in 2016?

First, our greatest danger is that we think we are so sophisticated and intelligent and our circumstances are so different that we could never fall under the power of an overwhelming and dangerous personality. Certainly, there are differences between our country and France, Germany and Italy of previous centuries, but also, there are great and frightening similarities. Like those countries, in the minds of many American citizens, our country has lost her historic identity. Our very soul has been compromised. From a position of world leadership, we have plummeted into disrespect and impotence. This has happened under a vast uncontrolled bureaucracy and the weak, divisive leadership of a cold, aloof president who continually makes decisions against the national interest and whose only concern has been promoting his ideology even when it is taking us to destruction.

Add to this a faltering economy and a government that manipulates data to hide the reality of that situation; add to this ever-increasing bloodshed in our streets from both foreign and domestic enemies, made so much worse by the unwillingness of the current government to be honest about who those enemies are; add to this an invasion of people who do not share our values, and the result is rage, hate and desperation. Those emotions mirror the emotions of France, Germany and Italy of the past.

Now, for our discussion, it doesn't matter whether the perception I described is true or not. What matters is that millions of Americans believe it with such ferocity that it brings blood to their eyes. This places us into a position of great vulnerability for the rise of an Over Man.

Let's imagine what such an American leader could be like. As in the past, because of his overwhelming personality, total self-confidence and willingness to do and say anything to accomplish his goals, compared to him, all other candidates, no matter their actual qualifications, will look weak and pale. This was true of Napoleon, Hitler and Mussolini. It has been true of every Over Man who has ever appeared to lead a country to destruction. It is true of Donald Trump. I believe that Mr. Trump is the American Over Man. Does that sound ridiculous? How could such a loudmouthed buffoon rise to great national power? Look at each of the three leaders that I've mentioned. Viewed before they ascended, no one could have imagined what they would become.

It is clear from his many arrogant statements and personal history that Mr. Trump fits Nietzschean qualifications. He views himself as above the rest of humanity. In the way he conducts his life, he is deeply aware that the rules of common morality do not apply to him. He skates straight through them. Though he claims to be a "Christian", there is no evidence that he answers to anyone but himself. He feels no need of forgiveness for anything that he has ever done. At most, he communicates a mild regret. God has no place in his personal equation, except to gain votes. To him, power exists for its own sake and he is the man who is strong enough to grasp and wield it. It is clear that he feels it is his right and responsibility to lead America. He views himself as our salvation. "I will do this for you ... I will protect you." Never have we experienced such arrogance, which sets him apart from every other serious candidate for President in the history of this country. The only category in which he fits is Over Man. Because they have no knowledge of history, Americans try to jam him into the only categories they know. This is a terrible mistake.

Having said all of that, I believe that this is Donald Trump's moment and he can't be stopped. To face him, the Democrat party has fielded one of the weakest candidates they could have chosen. Like an old garbage scow encrusted with a million barnacles, Ms. Clinton coughs and churns her way along, her only qualification being her gender. Her life is so compromised by greed and perfidy, she is such a liar, that even many in her own party can't stomach her candidacy. Donald Trump could not have hoped for a more vulnerable, but useful, candidate. Ms. Clinton is the perfect foil for all the hate, rage and desperation in this country. All he has to do is invoke her name and any serious scrutiny of his own evil life vanishes like a fart in a hurricane. Passionate stupidity filled with hate and rage directed toward Hillary Clinton provides all the cover that he could ever need. It feels almost as though the entire charade had been planned.

But there is another reason why Mr. Trump can't be stopped and it is even more disturbing.

Like Over Men of the past in their countries, and like no other candidate in recent memory, he personifies who we are and who we want to be as Americans in 2016. This is why we are drawn to him. Whether we like it or not, he is our ideal, a man who actually lives our dreams, our aspirations and our morality. We are not a "Christian" nation. The true American god of 2016 is celebrity, success and money. We worship the glittering power that they create. This is just as true in our academic classrooms and scientific laboratories as in our churches. It is just as true for conservatives as for progressives, for Christians as for atheists.

Donald Trump personifies our new understanding of independence.

He lives by his own rules, answering to no one. Whatever he chooses to do, there are no negative consequences. Whether it's a billion dollar business deal, or bedding a woman, everything always turns out well for him, including his children. Why is this so? *Because he wills it to be so.* This is his constant message of personal power and freedom to American voters. To a nation of frightened, selfish children, the message is irresistible. He will be our father. He will take care of us. He will make us great again. I contend that Donald Trump is both the quintessential American and the quintessential father of 2016.

Are you a progressive and do you think Donald Trump stands for everything you hate? Consider a few things: In a country that is increasingly atheist and agnostic all that matters is personal choice governed by an individually constructed moral code. Where did your moral code originate? You cobbled it together yourself from many sources and it is conveniently flexible depending upon "necessity". How might you apply it? Here's a small possibility. When you answer to no one but yourself, if you find it personally "necessary", you can choose to kill a baby in the womb because, by fiat, you have determined that the child is only expendable tissue. This is nothing but the application of Nietzschean raw power disconnected from any Ultimate Responsibility.

When your personal ethics are determined by convenience and desire, which you define as necessity, you are living your life in Donald Trump's ethical mansion.

But at least he doesn't want to murder innocent Muslims. He doesn't want to categorize them as expendable tissue. He only wants to keep them out. If it helps, think of it as an act of Planned National Fatherhood, like placing a huge condom on immigration. Our Father is only protecting us, his true natural-born children. Don't you understand? Our country can't afford any more kids.

Another similarity: Mr. Trump is famous in business for breaking his contracts and not keeping his word. He's famous for doing the same thing in marriage. Have you broken your marriage vows purely because you decided it was something you "needed" to do and then you justified it? Have you ever made a business decision that went against your "ethical code" because it was convenient? How different are you from Donald Trump? You may not like his moral code, but who is to say that yours is better than his or even that much different? Who has the right to make such a "moral" judgement and on what authority can it be made?

At rock bottom, the way Donald Trump lives is the way almost all Americans would like to live. We want success in every area and no negative consequences no matter what we choose to do. Of course, our selfishness is always mediated by the desire to be considered "nice people". That is one of the things that differentiates the average self-centered American from Mr. Trump. Over Man never worries about being considered a nice person. If he is nice or kind, it is because he deigns to be so, not because he considers it a necessity. But kind or not, he will accomplish his goals. It is unlikely that you have ever met anyone with such self-possession and confidence in his own power, who actually possesses great power.

Recently, I read a horrifying book.

It is entitled Hitler's Last Secretary: A First-Hand Account of Life with Hitler by Traudl Junge. Ms. Junge was only 21 years old when she joined Hitler's close, personal staff. From that point she was with him almost every day for two and a half years, ending only at the bunker. How would you like to work for an employer who was always kind and considerate and never critical, who never overloaded you or asked you to do more than you could handle, who was constantly concerned for your personal welfare? As an attractive young woman, how would you like to work for an employer who never used sexual innuendos, or made passes at you and who always treated you with the utmost respect? That was Adolph Hitler. He treated Ms. Junge like a daughter and tried to help her find the right young man to marry. He was her kind father, all while murdering untold millions.

While he was such a wonderful employer, Ms. Junge relates that every single thing revolved totally around him and his desires. But that was never because he insisted on it. He didn't have to. She relates that all those on his staff were overwhelmed by his personality. To them he was magnanimous, but they hung on his every word. To others in other settings, Hitler was a raging maniac, nick-named the "carpet chewer" for the way he could lose control like one possessed. In two and a half years, Ms. Junge never saw that side of him. Later she understood that he was two completely different people. The closest she came to seeing that other "person" were the few times when a topic was raised that Hitler did not want to discuss, such as when the wife of one of his staff expressed concern for the poor Jews she had seen being shipped out in boxcars. Couldn't Hitler do something to help them? At such moments, a flash of utter coldness would come into his eyes and the conversation would end never to be broached again.

In those two and a half years living in her protected, isolated environment, Ms. Junge says she never knew about all the horrors that were taking place in the outside world. For that she felt much guilt to the end of her life. So, remember this in the months ahead as you hear all the glowing stories about Mr. Trump from people who love him and who have experienced his great kindness. Over Man can be very kind indeed.

As much as Progressives share the real values of Donald Trump, at least they hate his public pronouncements and sense that he is a demagogue. Far more hypocritical and blind are those social conservatives and evangelical Christians who are placing their faith in him. For decades they have considered themselves the Keepers of the Moral Flame in America. They have taken pride in their ethical vision of what America should be. But the rise of Donald Trump is bringing out the truth of what they really believe. They are motivated by the same hate, rage and desperation as people who do not claim to know God. This is proof that what has been going on in so many churches for decades bears no resemblance to Biblical Christianity at all. The pagan god of success, prosperity and security has been painted to look like Jesus. Little wonder that now Donald Trump, one of his high priests, is being "baptized" as a "Christian" so good church people can pretend he is one of their own. (This is a particularly dry baptism even for Presbyterians.)

In addition to the preceding two articles, the following internet articles consider, as well, Trump's possible, or impossible, relation to Nietzsche's overman concept.

Donald Trump: Nietzsche's Superman? |Austin Carty | Aug. 11, 2015 | HuffPost Entertainment
"Nietzsche's whole agenda was to show that morality is arbitrary and that power is everything; in fact, his whole agenda was to show that the powerful determine what morality is, and that the crowd goes along with the powerful because, mesmerized by their power, they mimic their morality.

In watching Trump's popularity surge, it's hard not to see parallel relationships between Trump and Nietzsche's overman concept.

Trump Is Nietzsche's Last Man Not Übermensch | Frank Moraes | December 22, 2016 |
"For Nietzsche, the celebration of a man like Trump was the inevitable result of a democratic culture built on the virtues of ignorance and self-fulfillment."

The post-truth era of Trump is just what Nietzsche predicted | Beth Daley, editor and general manager | December 14, 2016 | The Conversation

"For Nietzsche, each perspective on the world will have certain things it assumes are non-negotiable – "facts" or "truths" if you like. Pointing to them won't have much of an effect in changing the opinion of someone who occupies a different perspective. Sure enough, Trump's supporters were apparently unperturbed by his poor performance under the scrutiny of fact-checkers associated with the mainstream and/or liberal media. These forces they saw as irretrievably anti-Trump in their perspective, with their own agenda and biases; their claims about the truth, therefore, could be dismissed no matter what evidence they cited."

How Nietzsche explains the rise of Donald Trump | Damon Linker| August 11, 2015 |The Week

"Ladies and Gentlemen, I give you Donald Trump, Nietzschean Republican. "No, I don't mean to imply that I think Trump sleeps with a copy of *Beyond Good and Evil* under his pillow. What I do mean is that Trump's style and substance (such as it is) grow out of a view of the world that overlaps in revealing ways with the ideas of the radical German philosopher Friedrich Nietzsche."

It appears then that all the aforementioned evidence fairly well indicates that Mr. Trump does not match Nietzsche's overman concept.

Yet, let me continue my exploration of this enigmatic man, from another perspective, perhaps in relation to the overman complex; namely, as mentioned earlier, his being a historic necessity.

SECTION III
TRUMP AS HISTORIC NECESSITY

PART FIVE

Revealed by Others and the Author

TRUMP
As an Historic Necessity of Events-to-Come

But is this "historic necessity" in any way related to the overman concept? We shall see.

Having given Nietzsche his due, and having studied Trump's **characteristics** in Parts one through Parts three; including the selected articles hardly supporting the position that Trump registered as Nietzsche's conception of the overman, nothing more need be said in any way or form as to whether or not Mr. Trump can claim to be related to the overman concept. As a matter of fact, it would be an absolute absurdity to consider him as one; since Nietzsche obviously included the following statements as indicative of the overman; which excludes any of Trump's interests despite whatever he or any of his devotees or cults may say to the contrary. Again, Nietzsche's affirmative qualities ascribed to his overman concept:

"Whom do you call bad? –
He who always wants to put people to shame."

"What is most human to you? – To spare someone shame."

"The search for truth is still the greatest (and only sensible) form of rebellion."

"You shall love beyond yourselves some day! So first, learn to love. And for that you have to drink the bitter cup of your love."

"What is important is the might of the soul that decrees death to death and dedicates itself to eternal life."

Considering Trump's exclusion from the overman concept, how do we account for Trump's following statements that seem to equate him to some kind of more-than-human stature if not an overman of sorts?

There's nobody like me. Nobody.

I've done things that nobody else has done.

There is no one in my age who has accomplished more. Everyone can't be the best.

I will save you. Only I can save you.

I'm the messenger, but I'll tell you what, the message is the right message.

I'm honored to have the greatest temperament that anybody has.

I think I was born with the drive for success because I have a certain gene.

I'm a strong believer in genes.

Do not these bold statements refer to Trump as more a world leader, than just the President of the free world; as though he were meant to change the business/political climate; and thus, the world?

"He's the great American icon!"
Trump: "Hey, why only American? Why not the world?"

In keeping with this ultra-statement, it appears that Trump, would consider himself more in the same strain as world conquering leaders, remaking civilization and culture, such personages as, Napoleon or Alexander in the Western world, and, perhaps no less than Attila (The Hun) in the Asian world, than as Nietzsche's overman concept. A man of world-destiny, no less.

Again, this bold statement gives rise to the thought that accepting the fact that Trump is nowhere near Nietzsche's overman-concept (considering all the evidence in this study); and that he, nonetheless has been crowned as an historic necessity by this author, then I have to ask, in what intellectual, pragmatic, sense is he an *historic necessity* – one, that he certainly believes he is, if asked of himself? Now, I think I struck the secret intent that goes beyond the Presidency of the United States (at least the Republican Party of it – for now). There it is, that Mr. Trump trumpets himself a conquering, destined, hero, intending to reshape the world into his towering elitist image of aesthetic, will-to-power magnificence.

Himself on His Aesthetics

1. Everyone knows how important beauty is to me. I always try to have it in my life. I hire the best people, find the most fabulous locations, and use the finest materials to make sure that every project I undertake is truly exceptional. Being surrounded by beauty makes me feel great; it enhances every part of my life, and I deserve it.

2. Beauty and elegance, whether in a woman, a building, or a work of art, is not just superficial or something pretty to see. Beauty and elegance are products of personal style that come from deep within.

3. My style is based on trying to make whatever I do breathtakingly beautiful. People react emotionally to my style; they want more of it. It's no accident that I'm so involved with beauty; it's my signature, my brand, and I think it's best to have it in spades.

4. Contact with beauty exposes successful people to an excellence from which they can learn, grow, and improve their lives. Beauty rewards people for all their hard work.

5. I love to take an undeveloped piece of property and turn it into something magnificent.

6. I don't do it for the money. I've got enough, much more than I'll ever need. I do it to do it. Deals are my art form. Others paint beautifully on canvas or write wonderful poetry. I like making deals, preferably big deals. That's how I get my kicks.

7. I look at things for the art sake and the beauty sake and for the deal sake.

Himself on His Will-to-Power

8. They have never seen anyone like me in politics. They have never seen anyone who is willing to stand up to the lobbyists, the PACs, the special interests, who all have way too much influence over Washington politicians. I am paying my own way so I can say what I want. I will only do what is right for our country, which I love.

9. I dealt with Gaddafi [former Libya ruler]. I rented him a piece of land. He paid me more for one night than the land was worth for two years, and then I didn't let him use the land. That's what we should be doing. I don't want to use the word "screwed," but I screwed him. That's what we [United States government] should be doing.

10. You listen to the politicians and it's as if they are speaking from a script titled "How Boring Can I Possibly Be?" They're so afraid of tripping on their own words, terrified that they're going to say something unscripted and go off message – that's the phrase they use, "go off message" – that they are verbally paralyzed. They'll do anything they can to avoid answering a question--and the media plays the game with them.

11. The basic difference between the politician's way and my way is that I've actually had to do the things that politicians only talk about doing.

12. The special interests and lobbyists ... I do not take a penny from those people. I'm paying my own way. So the old rules don't apply to me – and those people who benefit from those rules don't know how to react. At first, they hoped if they ignored me I would go away.

13. I never worry about being politically correct. I don't need to read the polls to make my decisions. And I don't see any reason to change my approach.

14. One of the key problems today is that politics is such a disgrace, good people don't go into government.

15. A lot of times when I speak, people say I don't provide specific policies that some pollster has determined are what people want to hear. I know that's not the way professional politicians do it – they seem to poll and focus-group every word.

16. I ask people to look at what I've done throughout my whole career. Look at how successful I've been doing things my way. So, they have a choice. They can pretend some impossible solution is actually going to happen, or they can listen to the person who has proved that he can solve problems.

17. I think I'm too honest, and perhaps too controversial, to be a politician. I always say it like it is, and I'm not sure that a politician can do that, although I might just be able to get away with it because people tend to like me. And therefore, despite all the polls that say I should run I would probably not be a very successful politician.

18. I would center my presidency on three principles: one term, two-fisted policies, and no excuses. For voters it would be a business approach, and the best one available in the presidential marketplace. I'd lead by example. And what I could also bring to the presidency is a new spirit, a great spirit that we haven't had in this country for a long time – the kind of spirit that built the American Dream.

19. I would never lie [referring to the American people]. ... I would not lie. I absolutely would not lie.

20. What do you have to lose by trying something new like Trump? What do you have to lose? You're living in poverty; your schools are no good; you have no jobs; 58 percent of your youth is unemployed. What the hell do you have to lose?

21. I have made the tough decisions, always with an eye toward the bottom line. *Perhaps it's time America was run like a business.* [my italics to point the nonapparent direction toward Trump's ulterior motive aims]

22. We need someone with a proven track record in business who understands greatness, someone who can rally us to a +standard of excellence we once epitomized and explain what needs to be done.

Again, I repeat myself. Does this estimation of himself (#s 1-22) have anything to do with Nietzsche's overman concept? Not in the least. As a matter of fact, Trump has no more interest in Nietzsche's overman concept than do "Jack and Jill. And yet . . .

It is the glory of the conquering hero – himself being such a hero in the victories of all his professional endeavors over the years all the way to the pinnacle of the American Presidency – that has always been Trump's primary insight, consciously and subconsciously, so far as attaining the great American Reach. Accordingly, Nietzsche's overman concept would be too personalized for him, beyond the range of his natural temperament, disposition, and intelligence. It is the world's honor of him of which he aspires, not that of man's honor.

Accordingly, I offer my following impressions as an attempt to tap into his state of mind, to capture as literary, not scientific necessarily, a semblance of his glorified self-image (up to the gaining of the Presidency of the United States) – in the hope that they will add to the reader's understanding of Trump as an impressionistic more-than-human man, which he, and his followers, his devotees, consider him to be no less than a supreme 'lord' among mankind – and so, considered wrongly by his devotees, to be in accord with Nietzsche's overman concept.

1. *I am of the flame of life; all else to me are ember, smoke, and ash.*

2. *I think among the stars in a black hole.*

3. *I fear nothing but failure. Ergo, I fear nothing.*

4. *They say I'm too aggressive. They're wrong. I'm aggression personified.*

5. *Why do I need stimulants when I'm my own stimulant.*

6. *They say I'm ego-driven; little do they know my psychological-ego is merely the means to my supreme-Ego.*

7. Do I believe in God? How could I not. I've been created, haven't I?!

8. Even the best turns monotonous to me until – at last! – the worst draws me to itself once again.

9. Good or evil; which is it for me? Good _and_ evil, I would say, with evil (I dare to admit) predominating when in conflict one with the other.

10. Being so super as I am, would I ever resign myself to the Love tranquility of mind and spirituality of a Christ, a Buddha? Never in this life! You may as well attempt to uncurl a dog's tail, or domesticate a shark.

11. I'm not a man of the people, but for the people – at least in the long run, historically.

12. What I have done, perhaps much to the chagrin and harm of others, is what is to be expected from a man meant to change the world in ways totally unexpected.

13. If you're going to consider me an autocrat, then at least place me in the gallery with the best of them: Napoleon, Lenin, Alexander, Attila – those who conquered for the advancement of civilization, besides for themselves. What have I conquered in that company? Business and political outspoken and out-acted diversity.

14. Am I a kind of prophet? You could say that; but drop the "kind of".

15. My basic creed is simply: Be _what_ you are, not _who_ you are.

16. Am I a genius? You'd have to be a moron not to answer that in the affirmative. But what kind of genius? Now, the answer to that question would be considered a kind of "riddle wrapped in a mystery inside an enigma".

17. Sensitivity is not one of my virtues. What, would you have me victimized by the soft-hearted, or hard-hearted ones?

18. Am I a part of a blind obedience to a corrupt culture of world dominance? In one way or another, I might say vaguely, yes; yet my mindset is far too impulsive, explosive, to be controlled to blind obedience to anything or anyone except to me – or to _Me_ – which I term "the Donald".

19. Yes, I do "sow the seeds of discord" so that circumstances turn in favor for me – and for _Me_ – and may I add: for _You_.

20. Who is this Me in caps? It is the Me that determines me in lower case.

21. A pun: If truth be told – if that's possible with me – I lie and lie for my truth; and ultimately, for Truth itself, whatever that may be.

22. Believe me when I tell you, don't believe everything I tell you. Is this a paradox, a contradiction, or what? You figure it out.

23. I know that I'm a true warrior, though not of the soul as a Jesus or a Buddha, nor of the mind as an Einstein or a Shakespeare – but, of the Ego-will of all warriors, with a smattering of each of their individual genius. Think of me like the fighting spirit of a Napoleon or of an Alexander, and the like – to take on the world and change it in my spirited image.

24. You've got it all wrong, people! It's not the ego-me that I presume as boundless, but the Ego-Itself unleashed in my own ego; its personality, you might say.

25. Ego-Itself, as I see it, is blind-mad for Its expression especially for the titans of humanity like me; ruinous, if must be, to Its servants (myself as well, I hesitate to say). Our success is Its success; but once It's done with us, our inevitable fall must occur by dishonor, decadence, heart failure, madness, whatever it might be, so that It may continue to reign in paradox, riddle, enigma, glory. My fall? It's coming, I'm sure. Age has got me by the tail, by the short hairs. I'm in over my head.

26. Do I have an "Achilles Heel? I would never have thought it in my blazing youth; but I truly believe it to be – not that anyone would surmise it: "the child within the man".

27. I am of legend, not of folklore like "Honest Abe," nor "I cannot tell a lie" like Father Washington.

28. People flock to me as those seeking a dream weaver.

29. How could I be bad, a destructive force, when what I offer my fellow men are such beauty and play of style on view?

30. Loyalty from others is as discipleship to my gospel. You betray my gospel, you betray me; you betray me, you betray my gospel. And what is my gospel, religiously speaking? Not, as you might think: "the kingdom of Trump is within you; not even the "kingdom of God is within you" – though that might very well be the case; but rather the "kingdom of will" is within you. Schopenhauer, the German philosopher, has it down, so I've been told. I love those Germans, as I've said.

31.   The touchy question is, Do I admire evil dictators, whoever they may be? Certainly not their person, and certainly not their horrors or madness; but as captains of "Satan" (that is, human Evil) they're as admirable as captains of God as to their attainments. And for these evil ones, they are just as tortured and "crucified" for their ways no less than the good ones, however it may appear on the surface of it. Imagine not being able to trust anyone, not being able make a major mistake without 'losing face'; of having to be always alert to a possible assassination attempt by even those closest to you; of always having to be 'on' – <u>more-than</u>-human lest you be thought as <u>all-too</u>-human.

I certainly make sure I do not fit this profile.

Besides, quite frankly, however more-than-human I profess to be, my all-too-humanness always seems to get in the way; though, wisely, I let that be known to my adoring public. I let them know, or more precisely, <u>believe</u> that I am one of them; just as fallible as they are. . . . Somehow, though, I just don't like that word "fallible" when I apply it to myself!

32.   When I'm told that I contradict myself, I always reply with our American poet, Walt Whitman, "Do I contradict myself? Very well, then I contradict myself, I am large, I contain multitudes."

33.   Be it known, my critics, all that you criticize regarding me, true as you have it, can only be half-truths, if not less.

34.   I take advantage of every advantage that could advance me as purpose itself.

35.   I know my larger profile is a sham to my largest profile of mankind.

36.   Though I am of historic necessity; here and now, I'm merely of contemporary chance.

37.   What I am in public is-and-is-not what I am in private. Try unraveling that of me.

38.   Mostly I don't like nor care for people; yet I don't feel animosity toward them.

39.   I'm a beam of light in a dreary life that's immodest at its least; that is my glowing gift to mankind.

40.   I bedazzle people with my light of hope – a hope that fizzles when my light departs.

41.   I'm bedeviled from all sides by people who believe they're the "end and all". They just don't get it that only <u>I</u> am that – though I'm not

really. ... Alright, I admit it: I'm fallible; yet, aren't I <u>something</u>, being fallible! It's like I'm fallibly infallible.

42.   Everyone knows that benevolence is not one of my traits. Why then do I attract so many lovers of me? Is it because I strike a chord of familiarity with them? Or am I the thrill of the unfamiliar? Or both? Or more?

43.   I know my ego borders on the messianic – as it should be, considering my world mission.

44.   My reach is boundless however bound I am.

45.   From the time I was a boy, I wanted to build, but first destroy in order to build.

46.   Of course I'm calculating as to what is in my interest and to my advantage. Who isn't. The difference between everyone else and me is that **I** calculate by instinct, by that rare extra gene only the very few have. Which is? Foresight; in touch with the universe, in play with the stars.

47.   My campaign in the ultimate? To rule my history for the sake of history.

48.   How much can my mind take in! I tell you, I feel it bubbling over, bursting at the seams, the whole world is gurgling in there!

49.   I am not deranged! I repeat I'm not deranged, however appearances belie me. Certainly not mentally. Derangement of the senses is another matter. As during my millionaire, "captain of industry" youth when I was drunk with myself, in a den of haze and daze, completely "out of it". But those episodes were far and few between, when I began to realize that I was sinking away from myself; and sinking is not my style. And here I am today firm in mind and sense, ever about my world task.

50.   My carnality keeps me all-too-human when I would be more-than-human. Both can be a bother to me at times; otherwise, I'm fine with being a man in the middle. ... though if the secret be told, the <u>more-than-human</u> in me beckons me on somehow, somewhere.

51.   It's true, only the rich can afford my best. On reflection, though, are not the rich as much a reflection of humanity as the poor and not so poor? It's not my role, nor possibility, to please every class.

52.   You ask, what my ultimate purpose is in life. That "ultimate" purpose is <u>out</u> of life; and so, has no answer otherwise.

And there he strides, believing, adoring, his monumental stature, not as an overman, not as a mogul, not as a President, but as an *historic necessity of heroic dimensions* that has altered the status quo of traditional, conventional, political/business, paradigms that have long served their purpose as a thing of the past.

And how has he achieved that monumental medal of honor?

First, my answer: By laying the groundwork for the future of mankind (intentionally or unintentionally? Consciously or *sub / un*consciously?).

> "Hegel's [19th century German philosopher] remark . . . 'Great men are instruments of impersonal social forces that lie below the surface of history; they bow before the inherent logic of events. Hence also science and philosophy play a limited part in it.'"

These 'great men' call these 'impersonal social forces' their destiny.

Second, A statement of my proof: As an historic necessity, Mr. Trump has publicly exposed his dark side, or all-too-human side, or shadow side, or instinctual side; or in a comprehensive word strife side; or even more severely, the evil side, of himself as no other businesswise or political public figure of such magnitude. Yet, even so, he could not very well act out all the way with his The Lie ideology:– some of which, includes the Wall fraud, the Syrian attack against constitutional protocol, the immigration debacle of 'separating over five thousand children from their parents with no tracking process" – being obvious in the public-eye as its President; after all, he has to "act out the role" of social and political morality/mores concerned for "his people".

So how does he disguise his real intent so that he can gradually reel-in his like-minded supporters by the hundreds of thousands for the ultimate push – whatever and whenever that would be? Simple. He employs and partners the sly, outspoken intellectual fop as chief strategist (that is to say propagandist) acolyte and private, aide, Steve Bannon to initiate his undermining bidding – which is to be explored in the next chapter.

> And now let me survey Trump, with emphasis on strife: his primary "evil"; that is, destructive, hard-natured, fighting side; devoid mostly of sensitivity, consideration, care and concern and affection: represented as his "The Lie" doctrine.

HIS DERIVATIVE LIES

[Selection-repeats from this book]

1. I think apologizing is a great thing, but you have to be wrong ... I will absolutely apologize, sometime in the hopefully distant future, if I'm ever wrong.
2. I'm honored to have the greatest temperament that anybody has.
3. I'm really a nice guy. I really am.
4. I'm really not a bad person, I have to say.
5. I don't want people to know exactly what I'm doing – or thinking. I like being unpredictable.
6. I don't have a racist bone in my body.
7. I'm more humble than people might think.
8. E-mail is for wimps.
9. I don't do it for the money. I've got enough, much more than I'll ever need. I do it to do it. Deals are my art form.
10. If you have to lie, cheat, and steal, you're just not doing it right. ... My career is a model of tough, fair dealing and fantastic success – without shortcuts, without breaking the law.
11. I would never lie [referring to [referring to the American people]. ... I would not lie. I absolutely would not lie.
12. They're not used to hearing the truth from politicians, but they love it, and they love hearing it from me.
13. Maybe the journalists' most embarrassing moment so far came when I filed my financial statement. I am the richest presidential candidate in history. I'm the only billionaire ever to run. I'm not accepting donations from my rich friends, special interests, or lobbyists. When was the last time someone running for political office didn't take Money? The voters know it – and love it.
14. I don't know who Putin is.
15. I have nothing to do with Russia whatsoever.
16. They have never seen anyone like me in politics. They have never seen anyone who is willing to stand up to the lobbyists, the PACs, the special interests, who all have way too much influence over Washington politicians. I am paying my own way so I can say what I want. I will only do what is right for our country, which I love.
17. I have a nasty habit that most career politicians don't have, because I can't be bought. I tell the truth. I'm not afraid to say exactly what I believe. When I'm asked a question, I don't answer with a speech that ignores a controversial subject. I answer the question. Sometimes people don't like my answers. Too bad. So

they attack me.
18. I think the only difference between me and the other candidates is that I'm more honest ...
19. Why do you think people tune in [when I'm on TV]? The fact is I give people what they need and deserve to hear – exactly what they don't get from politicians – and that is The Truth. Our country is a mess right now and we don't have time to pretend otherwise. We don't have time to waste on being politically correct.
20. It's [his feeling of guilt about his wealth] not overriding, but I do have it. ... I do have a feeling of guilt. I'm living well and like it, I know that many other people don't live particularly well. I do have a social consciousness. I'm setting up a foundation; I give a lot of money away and I think people respect that. The fact that I built this large company by myself, working people respect that; but the people who are at high levels don't like it. They'd like it for themselves.
21. I'm too busy to be devious.
22. I am somebody with a lot of heart. God is in my life every day.
23. In business I don't actively make decisions based on my religious beliefs, but those beliefs are there – big time.
24. Nobody has done more for Christianity or for evangelicals or for religion itself than I have.

HIS DERIVATIVE TRUTHS

25. People are tired of these nice people.
26. It's always good to do things nice and complicated so that nobody can figure it out.
27. I'm the Ernest Hemingway of 140 characters.
28. I'm a guy who lies awake at night and thinks and plots.
29. I use emotion for the many, and use reason for the few. [taken from Hitler's statement]
30. [Asked if he treats women with respect] I can't say that.
31. Women, you have to treat them like s- - t.
32. He [his brother, Fred Jr.] totally gave of himself. And I tend to be just the opposite.
33. I get bored easily; my attention span is short and probably my least favorite thing to do is to maintain the status quo. Instead of being content when everything is going fine, I start getting impatient.
34. [on being "a very shallow person"] That's one of my strengths. I never pretend to be anything else.
35. I was a very rebellious kind of person. ... I always loved to fight, all types of fights, including physical.

36. I'm really good at war. I've had a lot of wars of my own. ... I love war in a certain way. But only when we win."
37. I understand the military. I know the military.
38. I'm never satisfied.
39. The best thing about me is that I'm rich.
40. Sometimes, part of making a deal is denigrating your competition.
41. I want the assholes out of here. I want the incompetence out of here. I want people in here who are going to kick some ass. I want pricks. What I need are more nasty pricks in this company. Warriors.
42. ["It was the part of the deal Donald loved, that touch of moral Larceny."] This is one of the best deals I ever made in my life. I really, really whipped this guy, really took this sucker for some big money.
43. Controlled neuroses means having a tremendous energy level, an abundance of discontent that often isn't visible. It's also not oversleeping. I don't sleep more than four hours a night. I have friends who need twelve hours a night and I tell them they're at a major disadvantage in terms of playing the game.
44. Everything I do in life is framed through the view of a businessman. That's my instinct.
45. I am shaking up the establishment on both sides of the political aisle.
46. I have made the tough decisions, always with an eye toward the bottom line. Perhaps it's time America was run like a business.
47. That's true. [regarding breaking the rules of how candidates usually act.] That, I agree with you. They say there's never been anything like this.
48. I'm not playing by the usual status-quo rules.
49. I dealt with Gaddafi [former Libya ruler]. I rented him a piece of land. He paid me more for one night than the land was worth for two years, and then I didn't let him use the land. That's what we should be doing. I don't want to use the word "screwed," but I screwed him. That's what we [United States government] should be doing.
50. I'm representing the greatest, smartest, most loyal, best people on earth—the deplorables [the unfortunates, the wretched]."
51. Why are they elite?" [the enclosed wealthy, cultural clique] "I have a much better apartment than they do. I'm smarter than they are. I'm richer than they are. I became president, and they didn't.

HIS DERIVATIVE CONTRADICTIONS

[1]
Everybody kisses your ass when you're hot. If you're not hot, they don't even call. So, it's always good to stay hot.

I hate people that think they're hot stuff, and they're nothing.

[2]
I would tax people of wealth, of great wealth, people over $10 million, by 14.25 percent.
[Asked about his tax cuts for billionaires on CNBC:] I am not necessarily a huge fan of that.

[3]
I read a lot ... and over my life, I've read so much.
I don't read much.

[4]
I see no value whatsoever in believing ignorance to be an attribute.
I love the poorly educated.

[5]
We are the greatest country the world has ever known.
Maybe we Americans pump ourselves up too much.

[6]
Be tough, be smart, be personable, but don't take things personally.
When someone attacks me, I attack back. Hard.

[7]
New York is a great place. It's got great people. It's got loving people, wonderful people.
You know where the real jungle lives? Manhattan, New York city. That's my jungle and that's the real jungle. There're more snakes here and more things that can kill you here.

[8]
Nobody owns me.
I'm owned by the people!

[9]
I do not condone violence in any shape.

If you see somebody getting ready to throw a tomato, knock the crap out of 'em, would you? Seriously. OK? Just knock the hell – I promise you, I will pay the legal fees, I promise, I promise.

[10]
I'm an environmentalist.
Global warming is a total, and very expensive, hoax!

[11]
Women who get abortions should be punished.
Only doctors should be punished; women are victims.

[12]
Millions and millions of women—cervical cancer, breast cancer—are helped by Planned Parenthood. So, you can say whatever you want, but they have millions of women going through Planned Parenthood that are helped greatly.
But Planned Parenthood should absolutely be defunded. I mean, if you look at what's going on with that, it's terrible.

[13]
I'm a very untrusting guy.
I think maybe my greatest weakness is that I trust people too much. I'm too trusting.

[14]
[on being "a very shallow person"] That's one of my strengths. I never pretend to be anything else.
I am somebody with a lot of heart.

[15]
I cherish women. I want to help women. I'm going to be able to do things for women that no other candidate would be able to do.
Women, you have to treat them like s- - t.

[16]
I don't have a racist bone in my body.
I've got to tell you something else. I think that the guy is lazy. Probably not his fault because this is a trait in Blacks. It really is, I believe that. ... Don't you agree? ... [in response to the remark that that kind of remark could be damaging to his image:] Yeah, you're right, If anybody ever heard me say that ... Holy s_ _t ... I'd be in a lot of trouble. But I have to tell you, that's the way I feel. ... It's a trait.

Now that we have an overriding idea of Trump's dark, shadow, side, understood generally as evil (destruction); and that though he may be identified predominantly as an historic necessity, he nonetheless remains more a common man of clay ruled by his ego-sensual-self than as a world-conquering hero of the like of a Napoleon or Alexander who ruled the world of change. Period. . . . Or is this still yet an incomplete profile of the man?

For, as will be seen, we have not yet taken leave of Trump's not being related 100% to the overman concept!

Accordingly, we have to pursue the dark side of Nietzsche's overman concept; namely, it's evil: that is to say, its destructive side, which does not include malice or terror or hatred or abuse – traits which identify Trump – as we shall see shortly.

Accordingly, to complete Nietzsche's overview of his overman concept – as portrayed on the light side (pages 104-108), we must not shy away from what he also attributes to his overman concept on the dark side; namely, the destructiveness of evil.

The following passages by Nietzsche briefly complete his theory of the overman concept; including my selected, bracketed, comments so as to clarify his more possibly misleading meanings.

> "The concept of evil is dangerous because it has a negative effect on human potential and vitality by promoting the weak in spirit and suppressing the strong." *[its positive effect would be that it enlivens "human potential and vitality"].*
>
> "Concepts of good and evil ("morality") are culturally constructed rather than inherently "true"; different cultures develop different moral laws in order maintain social order."
>
> "I could dispense with nothing when I created the overman. His seed still carries all your evil and falsehood, your lies and your ignorance."
> *[Which is to say, the overman is the complete man-woman consisting not only of good and evil, but beyond them; inasmuch as **that-which** determines him as good and evil.]*
>
> "Every profound spirit needs a mask."
> *[to disguise his wisdom that man is multiple rather than absolute, is dynamic rather than static, is both good and evil].*
>
> "We imagine that hardness, violence, slavery, peril in the street and in the heart, concealment, Stoicism, temptation, and deviltry of every sort, everything evil, frightful, tyrannical, raptor – and snake-

like in man, serves as well for the advancement of the species "man" as their opposite."

"We imagine that hardness, violence, slavery, peril in the street and in the heart, concealment, Stoicism, temptation, and deviltry of every sort, everything evil, frightful, tyrannical, raptor – and snake-like in man, serves as well for the advancement of the species 'man' as their opposite."
[the opposite being that evil, in its way, promotes the good of the species].

"Under peaceful conditions a warlike *[over]*man sets upon himself."
[to destroy that of the ennui, decadence, and mire of too-long peace].

"Wisdom—seems to the rabble a kind of escape, a means and a trick for getting well out of a wicked game. But the genuine philosopher – as it seems to us, my friends? – lives 'unphilosophically' and 'unwisely,' above all imprudently, and feels the burden and the duty of a hundred attempts and temptations of life – he risks himself constantly, he plays the wicked game.
[of multivariousness, of the "derangement of the senses"].

"The strongest and most evil *[destructive]* spirits have to date advanced mankind the most: they always rekindled the sleeping passions – all orderly arranged society lulls the passions to sleep; they always reawakened the sense of comparison, of contradiction, of delight in the new, the adventurous, the untried; they compelled men to set opinion against opinion, ideal plan against ideal plan."

"I obviously do everything to be "hard to understand" myself."
[for dread of the unknown of myself].

"Objection, evasion, joyous distrust, and love of irony are signs of health; everything absolute *[without consideration of natural diversity]* belongs to pathology."

"To recognize untruth as a condition of life – that certainly means resisting accustomed value feelings in a dangerous way; and a philosophy that risks this would by that token alone place itself beyond good and evil."
[Both truth <u>and</u> unruth issue from <u>that which</u> determines both; and so, would dangerously undermine man's accustomed way of thinking.]

"Love of one *[person only]* is a piece of barbarism: for it is practiced at the expense of all others. Love of God likewise."

"If you have an enemy, do not requite him with good, for that would put him to shame *[His evil is his good.]*. Rather prove that he did you some good."
[by imparting the sight of his evil for the blindness of your own evil.]

What is evil? —Whatever springs from weakness.
[weakness to face ourselves as a complete human being.]

"But it is the same with man as with the tree. The more he seeks to rise into the height and light, the more vigorously do his roots struggle earthward, downward, into the dark and deep—into the evil."
[the evil which enforces, embraces, the fullness of our species]

"Deception, flattering, lying, deluding, talking behind the back, putting up a false front, living in borrowed splendor, wearing a mask, hiding behind convention, playing a role for others and for oneself – in short, a continuous fluttering around the solitary flame of vanity – is so much the rule and the law among men that there is almost nothing which is less comprehensible than how an honest and pure drive for truth could have arisen among them. They are deeply immersed in illusions and in dream images; their eyes merely glide over the surface of things and see "forms."

"What does man actually know about himself? Is he, indeed, ever able to perceive himself completely, as if laid out in a lighted display case? Does nature not conceal most things from him — even concerning his own body – in order to confine and lock him within a proud, deceptive consciousness, aloof from the coils of the bowels, the rapid flow of the blood stream, and the intricate quivering of the fibers! She threw away the key..."
[Our organic will to live ultimately undermines our rational will to think – about ourselves and everything else.]

Anything which is a living and not a dying body ... will have to be an incarnate will to power, it will strive to grow, spread, seize, become predominant - not from any morality or immorality but because it is living and because life simply is will to power ... 'Exploitation'... belongs to the essence of what lives, as a basic organic function; it is a consequence of the will to power, which is after all the will to life *[that is, all species of human, and non-human will (struggle) to live at its peak]*

Of all evil I deem you capable: Therefore, I want good *[and so, nothing more of evil]* from you.

Verily, I have often laughed at the weaklings who thought themselves good because they had no claws.

A belief, however necessary it may be for the preservation of a species, has nothing to do with truth. The falseness of a judgment is not for us necessarily an objection to a judgment. The question is to what extent it is life-promoting, life-preserving, species preserving, perhaps even species cultivating. To recognize untruth as a condition of life – that certainly means resisting accustomed value feelings in a dangerous way; and a philosophy that risks this would by that token alone place itself beyond good and evil *[that is, the Truth (purpose)of good and evil]*.

Against war one might say that it makes the victor stupid and the vanquished malicious. In its favor, that in producing these two effects it barbarizes, and so makes the combatants more natural. For culture it is a sleep or a wintertime, and man emerges from it stronger for good and for evil *[as the warming springtime revitalizes, reawakens, man's creative and destructive inclinations]*.

But every soil becomes finally exhausted *[goodness of losing its virtue, i.e. excellence]*, and the ploughshare of evil must always come once more [to restore goodness at its original virtue].

For all things are baptized at the font of eternity, and beyond good and evil; good and evil themselves, however, are but intervening shadows and damp afflictions and passing clouds.

When one speaks of humanity, the idea is fundamental that this is something which separates and distinguishes man from nature. In reality, however, there is no such separation: "natural" qualities and those called truly "human" are inseparably grown together. Man, in his highest and noblest capacities, is wholly nature and embodies its uncanny dual character. Those of his abilities which are terrifying and considered inhuman may even be the fertile soil out of which alone all humanity can grow in impulse, deed, and work.

It is, indeed, a fact that, in the midst of society and sociability every evil inclination has to place itself under such great restraint, don so many masks, lay itself so often on the procrustean bed of virtue, that one could well speak of a martyrdom of the evil man *[of having to disguise his evil]*. In solitude all this falls away. He who is evil is at his most evil in solitude: which is where he is at his best – and thus to the eye of him who sees everywhere only a spectacle also at his most beautiful.

What is new, however, is always evil *[up against what is old and dysfunctional]*, being that which wants to conquer and overthrow the old boundary markers and the old pieties; and only what is old is good. The good men are in all ages those who dig the old thoughts, digging deep and getting them to bear fruit - the farmers of the spirit. But eventually all land is depleted, and the ploughshare of evil must come again and again.

Where there have been powerful governments, societies, religions, public opinions, in short wherever there has been tyranny, there the solitary philosopher *[one who loves wisdom]* has been hated; for philosophy offers an asylum to a man into which no tyranny can force it way, the inward cave, the labyrinth of the heart.

In reality, hope is the worst of all evils, because it prolongs man's torments *[of not realizing their hopes]*.

With all great deceivers there is a noteworthy occurrence to which they owe their power. In the actual act of deception... they are overcome by belief in themselves. It is this which then speaks so miraculously and compellingly to those who surround them.

Most men are too concerned with themselves *[their self-interest and vanity]* to be malicious.

The civilized classes and nations are swept away by the grand rush for contemptible wealth. Never was the world worldlier, never was it emptier of love and goodness *[being fuller of self-love and self-interest]*.

I love something: and scarcely do I love it completely when the tyrant in me says: "I want that in sacrifice." *[of yourself for myself]* This cruelty is in my entrails. Behold! I am evil.

In laughter all that is evil comes together, but is pronounced holy and absolved by its own bliss.

Without cruelty there is no festival: thus the longest and most `ancient part of human history teaches — and in punishment there is so much that is festive!

A sure way to irritate people and to put evil thoughts into their heads is to keep them waiting a long time. This makes them immoral *[as a consequence of impatience]*.

This is the crux of the moral pessimists: if they really wanted to promote their neighbor's redemption, then they would have to resolve themselves to spoiling existence for him, and thus to being his misfortune [new-found guilt, shame, resentment]; out of pity, they would have to—become evil!

Some rule out of a lust for ruling; others, so as not to be ruled *[left to one's own lusts]*: to these it is merely the lesser of two evils

Man must become better and more evil *[against one's worser self]*.

And he who must be a creator in good and evil: verily, he must be an annihilator first and demolish *[outdated]* values.

That the world is a divine game and beyond good and evil: in this the Vedanta philosophy and Heraclitus are my predecessors.

From these passages, it is clear enough that Nietzsche includes evil as part and parcel of the overman complex. – inasmuch as it is a destructive force; and in the case of the overman complex, it is a necessary evil in that it is meant to destroy the historic 'Might is right' precedence in order to establish the new precedence, 'Right is might'; and so war. Think of it: Proponents, adherents, profiteers, of the former principle are certainly not about to peacefully, justly, wisely hand over their "pomp and circumstance". It would be unrealistic to think so; and so, war: war of words and laws, or war of arms and nihilism.

Such being the case and considering that the overman is conceived as mankind's next evolutionary stage of its human consciousness, which nevertheless retains its all-too-human self (his <u>humanness</u>: ego-self-sensuality) embodied in his more-than-human self (his <u>transcendence</u>: egoless-self-less-refinement), it is obvious that the overman's stature surpasses, the common man's status: his humanness.

In which case, the values and beliefs, ideas and ideals, of justice and wisdom, and their contraries, injustice and ignorance, will overlap with the overman concept.

'Overlap' in which way? Given the fact that both humanness and transcendent characteristics inhere in human nature, <u>conflicts</u> and <u>tensions</u> normally occur from that fact, such as the opposing results of contrary views, moods and events, regarding differences between right and wrong, between self-assurance and self-doubt, between ideals and realities, between hard and soft natures, between physical and mental traits to name just a very few.

Now, to resolve this "storm and stress", the despair of Shakespeare's lines –

"Life's but a walking shadow, a poor player,
That struts and frets his hour upon the stage,

And then is heard no more. It is a tale
Told by an idiot, full of sound and fury,
Signifying nothing." –

is what Nietzsche's visionary overman fairly much wars against; that is to say: outworn cultural, moral, religious, political values and beliefs; thereby gradually achieving, the <u>ascendancy</u> of justice and wisdom over injustice and ignorance —though, certainly not obliterating these latter. Thus, it is through psychological-moral-physical war (with peace interspersed) that event-by-event wins the ongoing victorious march of overman's <u>more-than-human</u> self over man's common <u>all-too human</u> self; or otherwise stated: man's transcendence over its humanness.

With this tracking of consequent future events the understanding that the historical <u>conflict</u> between man's humanness and transcendence transforms into a futuristic <u>balance</u> between the two. And upon this balance, mankind begins in earnest its slow, but sure, evolutionary conscious-transformation – from its "Might is right" paradigm to its "Right is might" paradigm – toward a 'brave new world' in its fullest meaning.

Even more conclusively, then, considering that Nietzsche's famous declamation "Man is a rope between beast and overman" (beast-man-overman); and that this 'rope' signifies the struggle, the back and forth pull, between the actual beast in man and the potential overman in him – Trump, as I see it, in no way concerns himself with this struggle. If anything, he already considers himself *there* without the struggle – though not as an overman but as an *overlord*.

And this point also eliminates Trump as Nietzsche's concept of overman. Yet, Trump's contribution is to <u>make way</u> toward the future realization of this concept.

Yet, as said repeatedly in this study, Trump's remarkable all-too-human <u>public disclosures and acts</u> (**!Lies!** being his hallmark of identity) as both supreme businessman and supreme, though inadequate, Plutocratic President of the United States, mark him as an *historic necessity*; inasmuch he exposed (and succeeded in doing so) his dark side, as fighter <u>against</u> men and events, however often in disguise – that mean-or-ugly-or-harmful-or-rebellious side of men and women that Nietzsche praised as reservedly necessary to offset the blasé, the duteousness, of too much weakening, stifling, boredom, of social, interacting goodness and self-proclaiming truths – witness our proclivity to offset, balance, these truths by our attraction to viewing and listening to the physical/psychological violence, insults, decadence, depravity, tragedy, horror, lust, available in the entertainment media that only the very few of us can resist, or to be indifferent.

In this achievement, Trump has contributed to, and so, opened the door to an enlightening vista of new moral, amoral, and yes, immoral adventures; for did not Nietzsche declaim: "The more good, the more evil." And in this sense, Trump would doubtlessly support the latter (evil); and in so doing, is he not as much a significant part of the overman concept – by his 'changing the rules': social, political, economic, business, political and psychological rules?! From here on in, the new rules will surely disclose themselves everywhere as an <u>openness</u>, a new burgeoning of consciousness, that have been mainly restricted, restrained, since, let us say, 'time immemorial' – that is, a consciousness, an awareness, acts, that signal *the gradual ascendancy of justice and wisdom over injustice and ignorance.*

In the end – and, in addition – Trump's contribution to man's future conscious advancement: his *historic necessity*, – is by his living, acting, and declaring, in the open, the dark side of our nature; <u>while at the same time, his being within the confines of the very institutions that he criticizes: business, entertainment, politics; somewhat like a Napoleon, or an Alexander being at the front line of their successful battles rather than apart observing and planning</u>. In which case, Trump has made it possible and probable that men and women in their slow momentum of social, psychological, and transcendent progress will be able to speak and act their minds (mostly more <u>discreetly</u>, with a more moderated aggression, gauged with understanding and wisdom, than with Trump) as never before. A "brave new world" it will be – I know you've heard it before; still, I might add, a needed 'delicate balance' to this brave new world to come. Then we will have an inner and outward adventure the likes never seen or known before – robots and all!

Thank you, Mr. Trump, for your upheaval, like you or not.

My final thought on this remarkable, though disagreeable, human being: "Such daring! Such madness! Such hubris! Such success!"

Good for, and of, you, Mr. Trump! However...

PART SIX

Trump from American Insurgent to World Emperor
Stated by Others and the Author

In this chapter, I venture to tackle what I predict as Mr. Trump's political domination of "Empire" within and beyond the spectrum of the United States. Let it be stated that all that I predict in the following <u>numbered</u> statements are basically <u>hypothetical</u>; though underlined with a kind of insight into Trump's human-transcendent mentality, as this book so far attests.

1

Let me set out on my exploration of Part Five's ending exclamation . . . "However!"

There remains two <u>glitches</u> left to be uncovered in this Trumpian mix; though they have been implied in this study all along; namely, Trump's ultimate <u>American</u> "secret intent" of not only cleaning the Republican Party of its 'swamp', as he put it, but of literally modifying the American government itself, its Constitution, and all else, under his autocratic leadership disguised as (1) making "America great again", and (2) of christening (the usual <u>religious</u> hoodwink) this so-called revolution as "Economic Populist Nationalism" – how, tell me, can he go wrong with such a homey, pragmatic, though misleading, nomenclature.

Yet, for all this scheming, let us take a look – even beyond this probable <u>American</u> takeover, at Trump's <u>furthermost</u> "secret intent", which stems from none other than his innate nature that makes it undoubtedly clear by his own words and acts that he could never be satisfied with just being President of the United States – nor of anything else for that matter: ("I'm never satisfied.") – at the probability that his ultimate political objective superseded not only any notion nor interest in being Nietzsche's typified overman, nor even being the President of the United States, but rather that his <u>ultimate</u> "secret intent" is to so strengthen his rule over the United State government as to make it the imperial center of world leadership with him being its mastermind at the mast, as its 'one and only' <u>emperor.</u>

To weigh in heavily on this monumental claim, I need only redirect the reader to reread Trump's own comments, and incidents, on it, which I repeat below:

But, first, I suggest rereading the following relevant quotations by Shakespeare that in their poignant insight says it all regarding the network of political intrigue within Mr. Trump's spider web (Pages 84-89) it is a pamphlet in itself.

And then, there are the following thoughts to consider in Trump's corridor of inuendoes, to repeat Theodore Dreiser's insight in his novel, *The Titan*:

"It is one of the splendid yet sinister fascinations of life that there is no tracing to their ultimate sources all the winds of influence that play upon a given barque [bark]—all the breaths of chance that fill or desert our bellied or our sagging sails. We plan and plan, but who by taking thought can add a cubit to his stature? Who can overcome or even assist the Providence that shapes our ends, rough hew them as we may."

"Who plans the steps that lead lives on to splendid glories, or twist them into narrow sacrifices, or make them dark, disdainful, contentious tragedies? The soul within? And whence comes it? Of God? [T]hat instinct for the essential and vital which invariably possessed him."

"Rushing like a great comet to the zenith, his path a blazing trail, Frank Cowperwood did for the hour the terrors and wonders of individuality. But for him also the eternal equation – the pathos of the discovery that even Giants are but pygmies, and that *an ultimate balance must be struck.*"[this author's italics].

And still further, You can be sure that Trump's trail can be followed to his alter ego, Napoleon, who has these comments to say related to Trump's sweeping hurricane. It's as though these thoughts, Trump fashions his own tirade of a career that led him to his conquering success – most of which he followed, some of which he should have followed were he a better man and mind.

"Religion is excellent stuff for keeping common people quiet."

"Religion is what keeps the poor from murdering the rich."

"Morality has nothing to do with such a man as I am."

"Greatness is nothing unless it be lasting."

A cowardly act! What do I care about that? You may be sure that I should never fear to commit one if it were to my advantage."

"Such is the general rule. Temperament, education, the accidents of life, are modifying factors. Outside of this, everything is ordered arrangement, everything is chance. Such has been my rule of expectation and it has usually brought me success."

"There are two levers for moving man – interest and fear."

"A man does not have himself killed for a half pence a day or for a petty distinction. You must speak to the soul in order to electrify him."

"It is astonishing what power words have over men."

"Force cannot organize anything. In the long run, the sword is always beaten by the spirit by which I mean the civil and religious institutions of a nation."

"Society is impossible without inequality, inequality intolerable without a code of morality, and a code of morality unacceptable without religion."

"I love power like a musician loves music."

"Power is my mistress. I have worked too hard at her conquest to allow anyone to take her away from me."

"I did not usurp the crown; it was in the gutter and I picked it out."

"I saw the crown of France laying on the ground, so I picked it up with my sword."

"Never depend on the multitude, full of instability and whims; always take precautions against it."

"There is only one thing in this world, and that is to keep acquiring money and more money, power and more power. All the rest is meaningless."

"To have ultimate victory, you must be ruthless."

"If you wish to be a success in the world, promise everything, deliver nothing."

"Friends must always be treated as if one day they might be enemies."

"I count upon taking [the French people] by surprise. A bold deed upsets people's equanimity, and they are dumbfounded by a great novelty."

"When your opponent is making a mistake, do nothing to interfere."

"The men who have changed the world never succeeded by winning over the powerful, but always by stirring the masses. The first method is a resort to intrigue and only brings limited result. The latter is the course of genius and changes the face of the world."

"Do you know, Fontanes, what astonishes me most in this world? The inability of force to create anything. In the long run the sword is always beaten by the spirit"

"Alexander, Caesar, Charlemagne, and I have founded empires. But on what did we rest the creations of our genius? Upon force. Jesus Christ founded his empire upon love; and at this hour millions of men would die for him."

"The world suffers a lot. Not because the violence of bad people. But because of the silence of the good people."

"Ten people who speak make more noise than ten thousand who are silent."

"Men are more easily governed through their vices than through their virtues."

"When a government is dependent upon bankers for money, they and not the leaders of the government control the situation, since the hand that gives is above the hand that takes. Money has no motherland; financiers are without patriotism and without decency; their sole object is gain."

"Put your iron hand in a velvet glove."

"There is a joy in danger."

"Success is the most convincing talker in the world."

"When you have an enemy in your power, deprive him of the means of ever injuring you."

"The herd seek out the great, not for their sake but for their influence; and the great welcome them out of vanity or need."

"We are made weak both by idleness and distrust of ourselves. Unfortunate, indeed, is he who suffers from both. If he is a mere individual he becomes nothing; if he is a king he is lost."

"As a rule it is circumstances that make men."

"Orders and decorations are necessary in order to dazzle the people."

"One is more certain to influence men, to produce more effect on them, by absurdities than by sensible ideas."

"A general must be a charlatan."

"You tell me that class distinctions are baubles used by monarchs, I defy you to show me a republic, ancient or modern, in which distinctions have not existed. You call these medals and ribbons baubles; well, it is with such baubles that men are led. I would not say this in public, but in an assembly of wise statesmen it should be said. I don't think that the French love liberty and equality: the French are not changed by ten years of revolution: they are what the Gauls were, fierce and fickle. They have one feeling: honour. We must nourish that feeling. The people clamour for distinction. See how the crowd is awed by the medals and orders worn by foreign diplomats. We must recreate these distinctions. There has been too much tearing down; we must rebuild. A government exists, yes and power, but the nation itself - what is it? Scattered grains of sand."

"Temperament, education, the accidents of life, are modifying factors. Outside of this, everything is ordered arrangement, everything is chance. Such has been my rule of expectation and it has usually brought me success."

"In politics nothing is immutable. Events carry within them an invincible power. The unwise destroy themselves in resistance. The skillful accept events, take strong hold of them and direct them."

"Among so many conflicting ideas and so many different perspectives, the honest man is confused and distressed and the skeptic becomes wicked. ... Since one must take sides, one might as well choose the side that is victorious, the side which devastates, loots, and burns. Considering the alternative, it is better to eat than to be eaten."

Then from my own perspective:

1. "... Yet, he never considered himself an ordinary mortal by any measurement, nor even an extraordinary man – that was always understood; rather his stance was that of a supreme man, a superman. By a 'superman', he would mean a man of super powers that transcended mere human powers; someone like a Napoleon, Caesar, Alexander, Lenin, who somehow or other

was in touch with the universal Mind, or Power of human events. Could it be he considers himself a demigod: a god-idol amongst men?"

2. "... The fight-lord, Mr. Trump portrays, has all the earmarks of this psychological conquest in which men/women worldwide will be subservient to the Man/Woman manipulative control through international inflexible laws, intoxicants/drugs, subterfuge, 'conspicuous consumption', endless comforts, public surveillance, religious subversion (all shades of Brave New World, especially) – the rule, not by physical force but by force of will; that is to say, basically by injustice and ignorance. What we realistic-idealists propose is just the opposite ideology: rule by force of character, by means of justice and wisdom."

3. Then there is his notable remark that must not be mistaken for anyone less than a "Roman emperor":

"He's the great American icon!"
Trump: "Hey, why only American? Why not the world?"

4. And the following still from a video that proclaims his self-idolatry:

This glowing image of President-elect Donald Trump, enshrouded in a white mist, glorifies his victorious entrance as demigod to his adoring multitudes. [Youtube]

5. Then, below, to prove that he is no mere mortal, or that he dared the loss of, or harm to, his eyesight, he dared to stare at the sun during an eclipse without eye protection – for only a <u>moment</u>! though; before having to put on the proper eyeglasses. On the surface of it, not much of a situation to claim Trump as an "immortal-mortal"; yet we can be sure that most likely what future readers and viewers will witness regarding this bravado act are only the photos of his staring at the eclipse <u>without</u> eye-protection: the god within the man.

Then, there are Mr. Trump's gospel of the savior, the redeemer, of the American people, who are in desperate need of his "coming":

1. There's nobody like me. Nobody.
2. I've done things that nobody else has done.
3. I am your voice. Believe me. Believe me.
4. I will save you. Only I can save you.
5. I'm the messenger, but I'll tell you what, the message is the right message.
6. I only have the power of persuasion.
7. Vision is my best asset.
8. I have amazing vision … no one else can match.
9. I think I was born with the drive for success because I have a certain gene.

2

It is fairly clear now that Mr. Trump, so far as his character delineation is concerned, dictates to himself, situates himself, in the company of such military/political world-shapers as Lenin, Napoleon, Alexander, perhaps Attila (the Hun), even Muhammed (militarily religious). And, as of Trump's character type, it will be evident as one reads along, that he believes himself capable of the same military/political alignments ("I love war. I **understand the military. I know the military**".).

Accordingly, however the worldly prestige Mr. Trump reigns himself as the American President of the **highest-ranking** political position in the land, still, he is limited, cramped, in his imperialistic worldview by being just (merely) the President of the United States. Too many restrictions from others of a much lower visionary, intuitive, insightful, caliber than himself derails him from that demigod stature. He views his worldview to surpass just the United States constitutional government. He has to be the (Roman) emperor from whom everyone and all events issue – if not directly, then indirectly; since, he alone has that "special gene" ("for success" of the highest order).

Be that as it may, he knows well enough that he cannot do this on his own visionary merits alone. He requires a Trotsky/Goebbels-like, intellectually-minded waring, front-line Lieutenant, to fight the war toward his ascendancy of world power and influence by means of political propaganda. And who would that individual be, we might wonder? You guessed it: None other than his crony and acolyte, his to be his general-in-chief, Steve Bannon, the loud-mouthed, viper-tongued, clanging, second-in-command chief: his civil unrest war-mongering propagandist.

Here is Bannon at his politically outspoken worst-like best:

> I think I'm a street fighter. And by the way, I think that's why Donald Trump and I get along so well. Donald Trump's a fighter.
>
> An elite is someone who's for themselves and not for the country.
>
> As long as you're a citizen of our country. As long as you're an American citizen, you're part of this populist, economic nationalist movement.
>
> Darkness is good. Dick Cheney. Darth Vader. Satan. That's power. It only helps us when they get it wrong. When they're blind to who we are and what we're doing.
>
> Economic nationalism is what this country was built on. The American system.
>
> We don't believe there is a functional conservative party in this country, and we certainly don't think the Republican Party is that.
>
> What we need to do is bitch-slap the Republican Party.
>
> "[P]olitics is war.
>
> I'm a Leninist. Lenin wanted to destroy the state, and that's my goal, too. I want to bring everything crashing down and destroy all of today's establishment.
>
> I am definitely going to crush the opposition. There's no doubt.
>
> 'National Review' and 'The Weekly Standard' are both left-wing magazines, and I want to destroy them also.
>
> The rise of Breitbart [News] is directly tied to being the voice of that center-right opposition. And, quite frankly, we're winning many, many victories. On the social conservative side, we're the voice of the anti-abortion movement, the voice of the traditional marriage movement, and I can tell you we're winning victory after victory

after victory.

This country is in a crisis. And if you're fighting to save this country, if you're fighting to take this country back, it's not going to be sunshine and patriots. It's going to be people who want to fight.

We're at economic war with China. It's in all their literature. They're not shy about saying what they're doing. Let the grassroots turn on the hate because that's the only thing that will make them do their duty.

I think Mitch McConnell (Republican Senate majority leader), and to a degree, Paul Ryan (Republican Speaker of the House of Representatives). They do not want Donald Trump's populist, economic nationalist agenda [author's underlining for emphasis] to be implemented]. It's very obvious. It's obvious as – it's obvious as the – it's obvious as night follows day is what they're trying to do.

With Bannon as the pistol in Trump's holster, this President has the right man to do his "dirty work", who would do his bidding without hesitation, without fear of reprisal: the execution of underground 'alternate' truths, that Trump could never expose by being foremost in the public eye; as the model of the citizens' welfare and benefit, safety and security – their "savior", as he called himself; as he 'adoringly' declaimed, "I love this country."

3

It is easy enough to see that all this politically undermining rhetoric aligns appropriately with Trump's own statements, though considerably more mildly reserved, yet just as misleading:

> I would center my presidency on three principles: one term, two-fisted policies, and no excuses. For voters it would be a business approach, and the best one available in the presidential marketplace. I'd lead by example. And what I could also bring to the presidency is a new spirit, a great spirit that we haven't had in this country for a long time – the kind of spirit that built the American Dream.
>
> I am shaking up the establishment on both sides of the political aisle.
>
> Perhaps it's time America was run like a business.
> [compare Bannon's specific Party: "Donald Trump's populist, economic nationalist agenda"]

Elitism is good.
[compare Bannon's statement: "An elite is someone who's for themselves and not for the country."

Our country doesn't win anymore.
[compare Bannon's statement: "We don't believe there is a functional conservative party in this country, and we certainly don't think the Republican Party is that.]

The special interests and lobbyists ... I do not take a penny from those people. I'm paying my own way. So the old rules don't apply to me – and those people who benefit from those rules don't know how to react. At first, they hoped if they ignored me I would go away.

4

Now that we're familiar with Trump's and Bannon's mindset regarding the gradual control of the Republican party and therein implanting Trump's own ideology, let us consider the following, likely, progression of their 'secret intent' considering that his administration continues favorably during his first term, and thereby wins the second term.

Consider that Trump (and Bannon) would storm the charge to re-invent the American constitutional government by undermining first the Republican Party by programmed lies, disguise and deceit – of which these so-called "revolutionaries" deem themselves unrelenting masters. Then, with their growing numbers of elected followers in tow, onwards they would mobilize their 'army' takeover of the other main branches of government until the federal government would remain sustained under Trump's autocratic reign.

Were we to consider that all of this monumental upheaval occurs without bloodshed, we normally would be dazed to have witnessed a major advancement in human psychology. We are then moving forward as a human species; a kind of evolutionary-conscious transformation! Great!

Yet we have to consider these thoughts that war in one form or another (I against you) prevails, bloodshed or not:

Bannon: "Politics is war." [no bloodshed here]

Trump: "I'm really good at war. I've had a lot of wars of my own. ... I love war in a certain way. But only when we win." [no bloodshed here]

"I understand the military. I know the military."

Be this as it may from one aspect – psychological rather than military warfare; not withstanding the military ever in the background should it be needed. Yet, from another aspect, we would still remain in the quicksand of our all-too-human selves. For consider further, for all of Trump's victories in this fabulous scenario, war still prevails, bloodshed apart, ("Politics is war." / Bannon); if not physical, battlefield, war, then psychological war inasmuch as there remains ever oppressors and victims.

The victims? Both the unaware/aware public who are duped and bilked into accepting submission lest they should protest, are weakened in outright fear and anxiety of losing their reputation, their honor, their job, their property, their savings, their credibility, their comforts – mostly by means of being sued, or slandered, or ridiculed, truthfully or falsely by a hugely monied and controlling administration, or by being slandered or ridiculed by the administration's supporters and mercenaries.

What do you think stands out as the main political platform of their mask of secrecy? Let me interpret it, as I envision it.

Simple. Dupe the masses with the idea and ideal of their advantage and consent by offering them a neat, impressive, inspirational governmental title. And what could be more enticing than the words "populist economic nationalism" for the people and by the people, and "Let us all make America great again!" Now you have them gullibly by the tail.

Having the blueprint of their insurrection laid out, both Trump and Bannon can next graduate their ideology toward their way to the God-Almighty "Crown". They will have both the government and the people overall under their control to activate their policies of, let us call "a spade a spade", in one way or another, that which has always been the historic case in democratic republics: a plutocracy; in simple terms: "rule by the rich" under the seductive guise of economic populist nationalism — most likely, with the backings of such "rogue" nations as Russia and North Korea especially.

The Trump-Bannon version of this form of 'world' government is that the people remain duped into thinking that these two elitists concern themselves with the people's welfare primarily, than for themselves (Bannon: "An elite is someone who's for themselves and not for the country.") : that is, their wealth and power are to be, in good part, justly and wisely distributed among the people (populism) – which, of course, is nothing but a myth; Trump and Bannon being the reprehensible persons they're stamped to be – And believe me, readers, they are more than proud to be considered as such. Similarly, compare Hitler's provocative statement: "We are barbarians, and we want to be barbarians. It is a title of honor. We are the ones who will rejuvenate the world. The world of today is dying. Our sole function is to finish the job." [from

Without Marx or Jesus: The New American Revolution Has Begun, Jean-Francois Revel]

I mention in the paragraph above the elites' wealth as being "justly and wisely" distributed among the people; which certainly prefaces an entire "brave new world" of governmental politics; which, which these two are obviously incapable of either imagining, initiating or maintaining; nor anyone else of their ilk, for that matter.

So, with this in mind, for Trump's boast that he alone is to "make America great again" is as meaningless as a 'chase after wind', a 'handful of sand', to put it metaphorically.

Both Trump and Bannon breathe an intellectual embarrassment of depth psychology, wisdom-minded philosophy, and humanistic science, that purport both the honor of wisdom and justice. So, please, you two political entertainers attempting to "change the world" with outdated ideologies that linger in the background of your sophistic rhetoric, as you both fume falsely as your lies hide behind a deceptive 'silver lining' of your pompous egos, we are on to you.

You trail so far behind in the past of 'Might is right' that it's practically a joke; beyond a past that is monumentally striving to be the present and its future of 'Right is might'; which I heartly proclaim in a caption as "the ascendancy of justice and wisdom over injustice and ignorance"; that is happening dramatically in our times 'all over the place' psychologically, philosophically, aesthetically, scientifically, socially, culturally, musically, the social media, dance, and on and on.

Think of it – at least, ideally at first: The wealthy sharing a good part of their wealth fairly and wisely among their fellow countrymen – not just this or that institution – for their good and benefit – not unwillingly, not grudgingly, but by right; politicians trained exclusively for their particular official position much the same as a surgeon or an astronaut, or an university professor. It wouldn't be expected of a primary-care doctor to practice surgery on a dying patient, or an airline pilot to man a rocket, or a high school teacher to teach a course in quantum physics – it would not be right. In which case, it can be said that perfection, the highest quality, consists of 'Right being might', rather than 'Might being right.'

The intuitive question then is how to attain this right frame of mind? Would it not be by the right education: that which is appropriate to both one's specific occupation, and one's disposition and attitude toward it. It would require a new kind of universally humanistic-educator to teach that right education.

So, to keep to our particular subject matter – namely, politics and politicians – I am forecasting PhD candidates qualified to train politically-bound politicians from lowest to highest office, all germane academic subjects (sociology, anthropology, economics, history, psychology, philosophy, criminology, etc.; as well as actual familiarity with the people of differing social strata, mainly as a journalist.

In which case, I am advocating *statesmen* in place of managerial politicians, whether they be generals, lawyers, businesspersons, the wealthy, the elitists, the "toss of a coin" candidates – that is to say, oligarchy.

5

AS A WARNING!

Here I end this forecast of ideas, and ideals, beyond the norm, the pale, of politics as it prevails in our times – and in all times, in one way or another; yet, it promises a new, dynamic, world of adventurous events of discovery as we slowly, gradually, experience the rising expectations of our humanity ever struggling <u>against</u> the gravity of our humanness – greed and lust – and <u>for</u> the transcendence of our being.

Yet, were we to daringly think of it, is not this perennial 'struggle', to better mankind, to reverse the 'might is right' to 'right is might' nothing but a futility: "a chase after wind", a 'handful of sand', as it has been throughout history to our times? – or as John Lennon glued it in the late 'Sixties':

> "The people who are in control and in power and the class system and the whole bullshit bourgeois scene are exactly the same except that there a lot of middle-class kids with long hair walking around London in trendy clothes. ... Nothing happened except that we all dressed up. The same bastards are in control, the same people are running everything, it's exactly the same. They hyped the kids and the generation. We've grown up a little, all of us, and there has been a change and we are a bit freer and all that, but it's the same game, nothing's really changed. They're doing exactly the same things: selling arms to South Africa, killing Blacks on the street, people are living in fucking poverty with rats crawling over them, it's the same. It just makes you puke. And I woke up to that too. The dream is over. We did our thing just like they were telling us. Most of the so-called 'Now Generation' are getting jobs and all that. We're a minority, you

know, people like us always were, but maybe we are a slightly larger minority because of something or other."

And to add to this incisive outlook, I can conclusively conclude for myself that for all my research, reflections, discussions, over the years concerning this book on Mr. Trump, all the authoritative books, articles, interviews, social media pundits, important and influential, thought-provoking remedies, projections, current and past – nothing fundamentally changes; might over right continues in its ego-maniacal, insane, patterns of the wealth-power elite continues on its cockeyed way of control of the citizens until now and then, the 'right over might' doctrine of justice and peace succeeds for a period; then back to the same "rotten-thighed" injustice and ignorance – witness: Trump after Barrack, Nixon after Kennedy and Johnson, King Charles after Cromwell, 'Congressional Government' after Lincoln, and on and on throughout history, mostly more than less :– the good versus evil perennial paradigm (as well as on a personal level the love versus lust temptation; and all the more that leads to 'strife in life').

But, back to the relatedly political scene. Why, I ask, would, should, anything change so long as the unjust and the ignorant dominate mankind by ego, lucre and force? Coming right down to it, it remains ever a matter of our groping transcendence being submerged by a long, outdated psychology's never-ending attempt to drown out any attempt of both personal and self-freedom. Yes, the mid-to-late 1960's rescued mankind's personal freedom for the most act; but not its self-freedom; which to our day still prevails as gasping, grasping, for air.

Considering the thrust of these thoughts, as far as I can think it, no real, lasting, change can rescue, free, mankind from its seemingly everlasting economic/political class-struggles, its existential malaise, no matter it be economics, this-or-that 'ism', this-or-that therapy, philosophy, religion, prayer, meditation, good-works, faith – without, I believe, a thorough, profound, sweeping transformation of our consciousness supported by a human-transcendent wisdom that predicts the ascendancy of wisdom and justice over injustice and ignorance; which believe me, is on our heels – look around you; it's happening everywhere; for one, read Marilyn Ferguson's masterful account of its breeding place, *The Aquarian Conspiracy*, and its continuing following studies over the years to our times.

This conscious transformation has no other choice but to occur, otherwise human stagnation will continue to wear down its, what I term, transconscious will to survive into the grips of the very few primitive-barbarians who will feast on the carrion of the static human mind.

Without considering the ultimate, ongoing minor wins and major failures of President Trump's managerial party, and of his lackeys, and of what he considers his historical legacy (Napoleon, Alexander, Charlemagne, et al) is that they do not, nor cannot, nor will not, recognize the "varieties of the species," so to speak; that is to say, the various distinctions and dynamics of psychological characteristics, such as Jung's introverted/extroverted human distinctions; or Plato's human philosophic/spirited/desiring distinctions; or the human distinctions between hard and soft natured persons, or the distinctions between the sociopath, the psychopath, narcipath (toxic narcissist).

To consider that all men and women are this-or-that betrays a very serious, almost ingrained, misconception of human understanding; noteworthily, in politics. Even Freud did not know: "What do women want?".

As a matter of fact, it would do the sincere seeker of truth, or of human understanding, or in a word: wisdom, a great deal of good to face and reveal this lack of human understanding, this exclamation: 'So much knowledge; yet so little understanding.' It would take something like a book on human *mis*understanding. And the underlying theme of such a book (or series of books) would emphasize the dawning of a human-transcendent wisdom and justice that would gradually – as it apparently seems to be happening in its nascent stages in our times – take the ascendency over injustice and ignorance.

A (if not the), for a start, beginning would be the reading and study of Plato's masterful ethics-political-metaphysical book, *The Republic*.

And then, what would follow from this advisory first assignment?*

---

*For those receptive to this forecasting of events-to-occur, you may request: "A CATALOGUE OF PUBLIC BENEFIT PRESS PDF BOOKS|BOOKLETS Complementary to the Wisdom of Human-Transcendence"

From thepublicbenefit1@gmail.com

IN CONCLUSION

As a final word (again): The reader might ask, "How does all this political meandering have to do with the two main themes of this study: Trump's character and Trump as an historic necessity"?

Well, is it not Mr. Trump's characteristic guiding principle of his ultra-superiority, of his mortal-godlike perspective of himself, innate to his temperament and disposition; that <u>defines his character</u> — The character that places his mighty ego foremost in whatever situation he thrives?

And as far as Mr. Trump being an historic necessity, has he not, accordingly, planted in the minds of millions of Americans that the American government needs to be overhauled; and so, to be made great <u>again</u> as was its Revolution and Constitution; and that he was sent to be the minister, the prophet, if you will, of that overhauling. And in so doing, as repeatedly stated in this study, to open the door to politically, and entrepreneurially "telling it like it is"?

Yes, he has, more *and* less – and I am sure he will continue to be during his time as President—mainly <u>failing</u> in administering <u>effectively</u>, with wisdom and justice, that overhaling (as did his heroes, Lenin, Napoleon, Alexander, fail, try as the might) but not in *initiating* the need for such an administration – though certainly not what looks to be another glaring 'old-hat' populist-economic variation of an elitist plutocratic autocracy with him as its magnificent ruler, if not, world emperor – like it or not.

The march of the ascendancy of justice and wisdom continues its way ...with, however, Nietzsche's warning, "The more good, the more evil."

Be wary, ever.

FINIS

BIBLIOGRAPHY

The sources of this book's quotations have been compiled and arranged, without editing, from both the internet and the following books.

- The Making of Donald Trump, David Cay Johnston / 2016
- Trump Talk: Donald Trump in His Own Words, George Beaham, / Adams Media, 2016
- Never Enough: Michael D'Antonio / St. Martin's Press. 2015
- Trump Nation, Timothy L. O'Brian / Warner Business Books, 2015 Crippled America, Donald J. Trump / Threshold Editions, 2015
- Trump 101: The Way to Success, Donald J. Trump with Meredith Mcliver / John Wiley & Sons, 2007
- No Such Thing As Over-Exposure, Robert Slater / Prentice Hall, 2005
- The Trumps, Gwenda Blair / Simon & Schuster, 2000
- Trump: The Art of the Comeback, Donald J. Trump with Kate Bohner / Random House, 1997
- Trump: Lost Tycoon, Harvey Hurt III / W.W. Norton
- Trump: The Deals and the Downfall, Wayne Barrett / Harper Collins 1992
- Trumped! John R. O'Donnell / Simon & Schuster, 1991
- Trump: Surviving at the Top, Donald Trump with Charles Leerhsen / 1990
- Trump: The Art of the Deal, Donald J. Trump / Random House, 1987
- Trump: The Saga of America's Most Powerful Real Estate Baron, Jerome Tuccille / Donald I. fine, Inc., 1985
- Playboy Interview, Mar 1, 1990

AUTHOR'S PROFESSIONAL BACKGROUND

Joseph Freeman

Educational Background:

B.A. in philosophy at UCLA

M.A. completed credits in philosophy at CSULA

Profession:

Educator, creator, and developer of *Studies in Meaning*, a critical-creative thinking curriculum, with his wife

Former high school teacher of ethics and logic

Writer of philosophic-wisdom

Author/ Compiler of *Of Pathics and Evil: A Philosophy against Malice; Christ: The Mystic Revolutionist; The Love Testament: Perspectives; Human-Transcendence: A Love-Wisdom; Beatles Spirit: In Their own Words and Music; The Lennon Testament: In His Own Words and Lyrics*

www.ingramcontent.com/pod-product-compliance
Lightning Source LLC
Chambersburg PA
CBHW060357080526
44583CB00012B/351